Breach of Trust / Abuso de Confianza

Ángel Escobar

Breach of Trust / Abuso de confianza
Translated by Kristin Dykstra

The University of Alabama Press
Tuscaloosa

The University of Alabama Press
Tuscaloosa, Alabama 35487-0380
uapress.ua.edu

Inquiries about reproducing material from this work should be addressed to The University of Alabama Press.

Manufactured in the United States of America

Book and cover design: Steve Miller
Cover art: *Viaje* by Nelson Villalobo, 70 x 50 cm, acrylic on paper; courtesy of the artist

Kristin Dykstra's translations have been carried out with the knowledge and permission of Ángel Escobar's widow, Ana María Jiménez (estate of Ángel Escobar).

"The Combat with the Angel," English translation of "Le combat avec l'ange," ©1958 by Lawrence Ferlinghetti; reprinted with permission of City Lights Books.

The paper on which this book is printed meets the minimum requirements of American National Standard for Information Sciences-Permanence of Paper for Printed Library Materials, ANSI Z39.48-1984. Cataloging-in-Publication data is available from the Library of Congress.
ISBN 978-0-8173-5873-0 (paper) — ISBN 978-0-8173-9071-6 (ebook)

para Anita Jiménez
for Anita Jiménez

Contents

Acknowledgments: Support for the Translation

The Banff Centre in Alberta, Canada, supported my translation of this manuscript with a short yet invaluable literary arts residency. Illinois State University granted a semester's research sabbatical in partial support of my work on the book. Supportive editors published selected poems along the way, often in earlier renditions: many thanks to the editors of *Lana Turner, Sirena: Poetry, Art, and Criticism, The Brooklyn Rail, Jacket, Mothafucka,* and *Sibila*—English for demonstrating interest in this writer who is almost completely unknown in English. (Interested readers may be interested in looking up Mónica de la Torre's small but magnificent set of Escobar translations). A folio featuring Escobar, with some poems from this collection, also appeared in *Mandorla: New Writing from the Americas/Nueva escritura de las Américas.*

I'm indebted to those who knew Escobar while he was alive and shared their personal and literary memories with me. They convinced me to translate this book. Reina María Rodríguez was the first to urge me to translate Ángel Escobar's poetry; she is committed to seeing poets receive more of the attention they deserve and mentioned Escobar to me in this light. Translator Udo Kawasser pointed out a copy of *Abuso de confianza* in a Havana bookstore at a time when US libraries held almost no editions of Escobar's writings at all. I encountered a widening group of people whose conversations with me about Escobar and/or specific poems and contexts enriched the project as a whole and encouraged its completion. Ana María Jiménez (Escobar's widow) and Soleida Ríos (his literary compatriot and longtime friend) deserve special mention here for their willingness to trust me with emotional and often painful memories. Carlos Aguilera, Pedro Marqués, and Efraín Rodríguez Santana— to whom the title poem of this book is dedicated—graciously discussed Escobar and their essays about his poetry with me as I translated them. Another poet, Rito Ramón Aroche, shared his experiences as a younger poet impressed by Escobar, and he told legends of Escobar that deserve their own future publication, be that as documentary or mythology or both. Nelson Villalobo(s), an artist and good friend to Escobar, sent photographs and memories that reinforced remarks I heard from others, as well as contributing his own insights based on their common aesthetic interests. Here I indicate two spellings of Nelson's surname to clear the way for future studies: while he lived in Cuba he used the spelling

Villalobo—and Escobar knew him this way, writing the surname "Villalobo" into various poems—but after Nelson moved to Spain, he began to use the "s," as "Villalobos."

My translations and commentary also benefited from the insights and encouragement I received over the years from Roberto Tejada, who is adept at translating difficult works and deserves special thanks here; as well as Omar Pérez (who highlighted Escobar's references to playing domino in "Funny papers" and remarked on the prologue), Francisco Morán, Juliet Lynd (author of one of the only other English-language resources out there on Escobar, and a wonderful reader of poetry and criticism), Tina Escaja, Dolores Labarcena, Rosa Alcalá, Leonardo Guevara Navarro, Daniel Borzutzky, Antonio López, Forrest Gander, Duriel Harris, and Calvin Bedient. All errors are my own. Finally, I'm grateful for the dedication of University of Alabama Press staff and the anonymous reviewers who dedicated their energies to this project. Everyone made it better.

Against Thingification (Or, On Becoming Inadvisable)

People who knew Angel Escobar enjoy arguing about which book is his best, and how each one will figure in literary history. I chose to translate Escobar's 1992 collection, *Abuso de confianza* (*Breach of Trust*), because other writers in Cuba described it to me as the most devastating work of his generation.

This is the first of Escobar's books to appear in English translation, so it introduces him to readers of English as a poet of dissent, in the broadest and most generous sense: *Breach of Trust* inveighs against forms of thingification shaping the modern world. He explicitly places the term "thingification" into his opening text, his "damned enigmatic harangue." It is one of the most challenging pieces in the book. Entitled "Broken mind," it is a poetic manifesto synthesizing an array of images and ideas while parsing selfhood through otherness in the spirit of Arthur Rimbaud, who wrote in 1871, "I is someone else" (366). At the climax of his prologue Escobar teeters between an emphatic NO and a fragile yes, foreshadowing the spiral of negations and affirmations that characterize the book as a whole.

Throughout the prologue, Escobar draws the past into his present. One point defining his long historic span dates to the colonization of the Americas, signaled through an appearance by the Taíno *cacique* (chieftain) Hatuey. Originally from Hispaniola, Hatuey encouraged indigenous peoples to reject the Spanish forces in the Caribbean, and their teachings too. In 1512, the Spanish burned him at the stake in Cuba. This ancestral figure has moved from history into mythology, in the sense that Hatuey's name is now shorthand for resistance and martyrdom in the Caribbean. Escobar's poetry is all the more powerful when understood in dialogue with this cultural backdrop. Even more pressing for this first translation of a book-length collection into English: in the wake of his 1997 suicide, Escobar himself is making a transition from marginalized historical personage into a mythologized icon in the island's literary pantheon. This passage of the poet into mythology is most comprehensible in counterpoint to the iconic figures and legacies of poetic resistance that he synthesizes in *Breach of Trust*.

Hatuey's emblematic story appears within *The Devastation of the Indies*, the famous call by Father Bartolomé de las Casas (1484-1556) to examine the violence of conquest in the Americas. Las Casas tells that when Hatuey was tied to the stake, a Franciscan friar informed him that he could still embrace Christianity. Hatuey asked if Christians all went to heaven; and when the friar replied yes, Hatuey said he would prefer to go to Hell. The tale of the defiant cacique insistently reminds readers not only of his death, or of the violence with which European colonization arrived in the Caribbean, but also of a competing reality: that tales of resistance are themselves life-giving.

Centuries after Hatuey's death, Martinique's Aimé Césaire (1913-2008) famously penned the equation "Colonization = 'Thingification'" in his *Discourse on Colonialism*, shorthand for the dehumanization and wide-ranging destruction of colonial enterprise (42). Césaire not only asserted the relevance of African diasporic experiences of thingification, but examined the broader condition of colonial violence on social relations. Explicitly aware of these cultural legacies, Escobar launches his own contemporary NO in response to sorrows that are inseparably historical and personal.

Escobar was born in 1957, toward the end of the decade when Césaire's *Discourse on Colonialism* appeared in print. His life began in eastern Cuba, in the mountainous agricultural province of Guantanamo. In his early childhood the family lived near a tiny rural village called Sitiocampo. As an adult, Escobar would remember that he came from a place so small it didn't appear on maps. Geographical marginalization was compounded with other challenges, such as legacies of poverty and racial discrimination. Escobar's family, who counted slaves among their ancestors, struggled with privation. The lands his family worked had long been associated with a history of hunger and difficult living.

As a student Escobar took a special interest in the theater, which would become the focus of his educational degrees. In 1977, he won an award for poetry, a national prize designated for emerging writers. He followed a pattern shared by many people from the island's eastern, rural provinces in the late twentieth century: he moved to the urban west, to the city of Havana, in search of opportunities. There Escobar made himself the author of many more collections of poetry, a book of short stories, and a play. Pursuing readings and conversations about criticism and theory, as well as world literatures and visual art, he incorporated Havana's cosmopolitan cultural influences into his repertoire. While he spent time close to the city's historic center, he also lived part of his life in the enormous housing community at Alamar, a development located on the eastern outskirts of Havana that has housed displaced and marginalized peoples. As Escobar connected with diverse cultural communities around the greater Havana area over the years, he earned a reputation as a restless, troubled, powerful poet.

His literary career lasted only two decades. Escobar took his own life in 1997 by jumping off a building, and it was not his first attempt. Today, his work and death resonate with writers and critics of different affiliations and tastes, perhaps the reason that copies of his *Poesía Completa* (*Collected Works of Poetry*, released by Ediciones UNIÓN in 2006) can still be found in Havana bookstores despite economic circumstances severely restricting print runs of most contemporary poetry collections.

Over the course of his books Escobar played himself out like a kaleidoscope, continuously rearranging shards of lines, images, and lives into startling new arrays. *Breach of Trust* is his tragic masterpiece, synthesizing disparate elements with assurance and musicality. Probably influenced by Escobar's gift for synthesis, some critics claim that he displays no clear rejection of a prior generation or style. Instead they place him in "a postmodern geography in which distinct poetic tendencies are superimposed without discrimination": the poet selects the most interesting elements of many traditions to incorporate into his own body of work ("una geografía posmoderna en la que se superponen las distintas tendencias poéticas sin discriminación"; Esteban and Salvador xxxix).

Summarizing a different and more specific line of criticism that has emerged around his career, María Lucía Puppo distinguishes three phases in Escobar's writing. His early books, which were celebrated and promoted by Cuba's National Union of Artists and Writers, display lyricism of a relatively straightforward and colloquial sort. Seen in retrospect, though, they contain the seeds of Escobar's eventual drift away from the conversationalist style popular at that time. When he composed *La vía pública*, first published in 1987, he entered a distinct new stage in which his poetry became recognizable as profoundly transgressive expression. *Breach of Trust* appeared five years later. It displays Escobar's roots in colloquial speech but, in keeping with the second stage of his work, crosscuts everyday imagery with competing stylistics and a stronger sense of irony. For Puppo and others, the aesthetic complexity of *Breach of Trust* positions it at the pinnacle of his second period of writing. *Breach of Trust* would be followed by three final collections comprising his third period, two of them edited after his death. In this series of mature works, Escobar built a lasting home in an abject lyrical tradition.

Breach of Trust projects many contrasts. Writer Carlos Aguilera suggests that to fully appreciate these poems, readers should keep Escobar's extensive experience with the theater in mind when reflecting on the contrasting tonalities of his poems. Aguilera depicts Escobar's speakers as marionettes jerked around a stage, their comic energies indivisible from the tragic scenarios that frame them. Abrupt, assertive rhythms of the street punctuate the poems alongside eruptions of baroque phrasing, which are meaningful in their luxuriance of sound and sudden density.

In Escobar's prologue "Broken mind" alone, the reader encounters a series of specific oppositions: ecstatic and dystopian visions, bumpiness and fluidity of expression, juxtapositions of elite and popular cultures, the highs of flight and the lows of falls. The prologue grows slippery and flirts with unintelligibility. A voice warns the reader that it will resist behaviors perceived to be reasonable, *advisable*: "I don't reason with the reasonable reason of the other, the other ones."[1] Yet the prologue offers the reader accessible entry points too, as in terse statements about suffering. Escobar also touches down in critical and poetic conversations before he takes off again in search of (or in a theatrical rendition of?) a poet's transcendent vision. See for example his citation of the essay "Kitsch y objeto" (Kitsch and Object), by Abraham Moles and Eberhard Wahl, or his adoption of the question from Yehuda Halevi, "It is ill: when will it be cured?" Can a poetic embrace of irrationality, of the outcast, give comfort when rationalism fails the modern world?

Translating the action of *Breach of Trust* into English for the first time has been a particularly complicated process due to the minimal attention granted to date to Escobar's work outside Cuba, especially in English-language circles. Many poets and translators research the literary works they intend to translate, and they consult scholarship and previous translations while developing their own presentations. In this case, there were few resources as I began. Fortunately a book of short essays celebrating Escobar's life had appeared in Cuba, and more detailed scholarship is in progress now. I anticipate that the discrepancy between his positive literary reputation and the dearth of contextual resources will continue to change for the better in the future.

Another helpful approach for translators is to discuss the work with the author, but that was absolutely out of the question in this case.

Ángel Escobar was deceased before I came to his book. Instead I've collected what research materials I could find, translating several short Spanish-language essays by his Cuban colleagues into English and referring to others here, in order to trace the beginnings of a more extensive and increasingly international archive about this impressive writer. I have also heard innumerable stories about Escobar. Since there can be a fine line between storytelling and archive—the oral and written contexts surrounding a poet—I've chosen to include comments here referring to personal interactions and some of the thoughtful, albeit undocumented, remarks I heard.

All manner of discoveries over time affected the language of the translation I offer here. For example, I developed a sense for certain sound qualities that represent a crucial element of Escobar's delivery, and so I tilted toward sonorous choices in my translation of his book. I discarded some literal or obvious options in order to evoke a more multileveled experience of his poetics. Meanwhile his rhythms are complex. I decided not to duplicate them stress for stress every time, instead seeking to generate English versions that would be alternately assertive and hesitant, musical, exploring the tension created when flows meet breaks. I was also influenced by personal, historical, and literary contexts, because *Breach of Trust* presents interwoven, knotted, evasive and/or multivalent meanings. Some poems led me toward context relatively quickly. At other times Escobar's fellow poets and family members, as well as critics intimately familiar with Escobar and his work, shared new perspectives with me that changed my understanding of a piece. And just as I was completing final preparations on the manuscript another poet, Duriel Harris, reminded me of the marvelous aesthetic and intellectual density of the thingification Escobar re/creates in reference to Césaire's term. As she told me about her performance piece entitled *Thingification*, then in progress, Duriel caused related ideas to click into place for me. There will surely be future reflections on the impact of African diasporic literature on Escobar's career, as well as reflections on the relevance of his writing to topics such as *mestizaje*, the histories of suppressed and public expression from Afro-Cuban populations in Cuba, the cultural dynamics of flow and transformation that Fernando Ortiz famously named "transculturation," and the relationships between Escobar's literature and popular culture. But these connections have yet to be traced more fully, and English-language readers will best be able to participate after additional books by Escobar are translated. In this introduction I'll present more general background information about Escobar and his writing, framed through a set of topics pertinent to *Breach of Trust*.

Merging personal and collective meditations, *Breach of Trust* is his indictment of historical forces spanning Latin America. It portrays lacerations left on bodies and minds by a violent century, and by the longer modernity of the Americas containing that century.

Ghosts

Breach of Trust is a haunted text. In this sense it's a good introduction to Escobar's career as a whole, in which foundational tragedy served as a recurrent drumbeat. Escobar and his siblings experienced extreme violence early in their lives, an incident that appears in both open and coded terms in his books: his mother was stabbed to death when he was only a child. Later the death of his youngest brother would add to Escobar's profound sense of loss.

Another factor that affected Escobar's daily life and mature writing was illness, which surfaces openly in the subject matter of *Breach of Trust*. His schizophrenia intensified during the years in which he composed this collection. Poems such as "Hospitals," "Guests," "Funny Papers," and "The four stories" display literal connections to that lived reality.

Commentators who knew Escobar during his lifetime highlight his references to pain and sorrow across the larger body of his work, referring alternately to recurring themes in his poetry and to their memories from his daily life as a writer. Images such as the splinter, both noun and verb, appear frequently throughout his poems (Martín Hernández 49–50). His fellow poet Pedro Marqués de Armas, who provided medical treatment to Escobar over the years, remembers the patient taking ironic attitudes toward death as a means for survival as his condition worsened.[2] Efraín Rodríguez Santana, who has worked extensively with Escobar's writing, sees in the later poetry "an extensive journey through spaces of the schizophrenic self, condemned to the accident of hypersensibility and surrounded by people invested in normality" ("un recorrido vasto por zonas del hombre esquizofrénico, condenado al percance de la hipersensibilidad entre hombres interesados en la normalidad" [2002: 9]). The speakers in Escobar's later poetry experience hostility emanating not only from external forces, but increasingly from inside themselves, as well as from forces difficult to locate with any precision.

From the home, tragedy leaks into the city—or is it the other way around? Personal and public, domestic and political realms merge. Puppo highlights Escobar's dystopic cityscapes: urban space is a meeting ground for his "social commitment, the great questions (philosophical, political, aesthetic), and the misfortunes figuring in his personal mythology: the misery and terror he experienced during his childhood, his mother's death at the hands of his father, his marginalization as a black man, the schizophrenia that finally steered toward the poet's suicide" ("el compromiso social, las grandes preguntas [filosóficas, políticas, estéticas] y las desdichas de la mitología personal: la miseria y el terror experimentados en la infancia, la muerte de la madre a manos del padre, la marginación por ser negro, la esquizofrenia que finalmente derivó en el suicidio del poeta," 226). In *Breach of Trust* Escobar gives glimpses of a city only in murmuring fragments, while a sensation of claustrophobia invades domestic interiors, leaving the speakers no recourse to safety.

Literary Ghosts

Escobar sets up tensions between self and other in his poems to articulate the internal conflicts of his illness—a self at risk in its dialogue with other selves. A sophisticated reader, he also used this strategy to accomplish other purposes. Intertextuality becomes one of his key mechanisms for entering and recreating cultural and intellectual communities.

Readers will see that many writers serving this function in Escobar's poems come from other parts of the world—Villon, Borges, Shakespeare, Carroll, and more. Their presences serve polarities of fragmentation and unity, which in turn bring tension and variety to the collection. It is particularly gratifying to read Rimbaud's "The Blacksmith," with its take on revolutionary enunciation, in dialogue with Escobar's longer poems in this book.

Another iteration of intertextuality in *Breach of Trust* involves Cuban poets and enters dialogues well known in the island's literary history. "Another text about another proof and another proof" portrays the balancing act of merging with a tradition while constructing one's own distinct voice and contribution. Escobar's famous Cuban predecessor named in this poem, José Lezama Lima, wrestled with the same poetic challenge in "The Death of Narcissus," to which Escobar refers with his quotation about Danaë and the Nile. Lezama's poem is the site of an encounter in which he establishes connections with his poetic ancestors, particularly the French symbolists Valery and Mallarmé. The poem demonstrates Lezama's struggle to achieve his own voice in the process. That struggle is inseparable from self-loss, forming a central opposition between presence and absence also operative in Escobar's riff on the piece. "It is crucial to Lezama's ideology," Ben Heller points out, "that an apprehension of the image of the self be achievable only through death, a drowning (precipitation) in the waters of the other" (54). Escobar places himself into this lineage, weaving lines and characters from Lezama's poems into the fabric of his own creation, merging self with other, life with death. In my translation, I've emulated his meticulous intermingling of self and other by quoting corresponding lines from English editions of Lezama's poetry. For example, the line "I insist on someone's pressing arrival" is drawn from "Pavilion of Nothingness," Roberto Tejada's English translation of the 1976 Lezama poem "Pabellón del vacío" (Lezama 2005).

As Escobar appropriates Lezama's image, there is a second cloud of meaning that envelops the predecessor's name. A now-canonical poet and commentator in island culture, Lezama is associated with a second literary mode of blending selves and others, a way of seeing that is steeped in histories of the Americas. Lezama's theory of the New World Baroque describes a powerful hybridity and situates it in the service of what he called a Counter-Conquest, rejecting notions that New World writers remain derivative when making work referencing European culture. Here, the "survival of Otherness piggybacking on the unsuspecting signs of Empire" asserts the diversity and influence exerted by the New World in all its historical and uncontrollable forms—a vision extending Cuban and Caribbean resistance through literature (Salgado 324).

Moving farther back in time: Escobar engages the island canon in his late poems by riffing on work by José Martí, as in the example of "Cuba y la noche"("Cuba and the night"). Martí remains the ultimate symbol of literary canonicity. His image as poet is fully encoded with resistance through his battle for a Cuban nation, which concluded with a most revolutionary martyrdom. More specifically, Martí was not only a great poet, still celebrated across Latin America for *Ismaelillo* (1882) and *Versos Sencillos* (1891). He was also a journalist and an organizer in the nineteenth-century movement for Cuban independence from Spain. He died in battle in 1895, becoming a martyr in the national cause.

As in the example from Lezama, engagement of poetic tradition around Martí involves confrontation with death. The title of Escobar's poem "Cuba and the night" comes from Martí's poem "Dos patrias," which opens with the lines, "I have two homelands: Cuba and the night. / Or are the two one?" ("Dos patrias tengo yo: Cuba y la noche. / O son una las dos?") The speaker faces division, juxtaposition and death in the poems past and present. Martí's literal death in battle at Dos Ríos has long given this particular poem about exile and longing extra symbolic weight by bringing Cuba and the night together in the retrospective vision of his readers: "Love of country and love of death drove him inexorably to that place and moment where all would acquire a meaning too transcendental to express with mere words. Death sealed life and poetry as a unit" (González Echevarría x). Presented as a widow in Martí's poem, Cuba becomes a wife in Escobar's reply, and she is the putative source of his poetry. In his response to Martí, Escobar dramatizes the process of coming to death in the homeland and signals the significance of grieving to an ethics and literature of nationhood. [3]

While preparing this bilingual edition, I heard anecdotes highlighting another aspect of canonicity, the staging of the marginalized other in confrontation with his exclusion from cultural authority. Some writers recalled that Escobar was sensitive to teasing about his education and origins, particularly when he mispronounced words or names in art circles after he came to Havana, or when he spoke with a strong eastern accent. Artist Nelson Villalobo, a close friend to Escobar, told me a more specific memory dating to circa 1975: in morning assemblies for the National School for Visual Art, Escobar read poems by José Martí, and other students laughed at his accent.[4] But he persisted. Escobar was pressured to show he could perform in more elite cultural modes, and *Breach of Trust* shows him demonstrating mastery of an international, western-oriented poetry canon with a defiance all his own.

With Escobar's own tragic death less than a decade after *Breach of Trust* was published, readers again arrive at poetry through the emotional overtones of the poet's literal disappearance. From Hatuey to Martí to Lezama to Escobar, *Breach of Trust* revives legacies of martyrdom through a parade of historical figures who have become larger than life—and larger than death.

Nation: A Changing Theater

In 1959, when Escobar was still a tiny child, dramatic events of the Cuban Revolution changed the potential trajectory of his life. Cuba's Revolution and the government it established represent a significant intervention into island history. Its leaders sought to restructure Cuban society to create a more equitable world; their visions were utopian, and so was much of the language used to motivate citizens to participate in the social programs they created. Many central aspects of Escobar's career make sense largely in relation to particular times and places in post-1959 island history, and this includes elements of *Breach of Trust*.

Seeking to reach families long marginalized in island life, the government led by Fidel Castro designed initiatives intended to remedy the long history of rural poverty on the island and reduce some forms of discrimination against black Cubans, goals affecting Escobar and his family. In this battle to overturn legacies of colonization/thingification (which Césaire had described as destructive to both the colonizers and the colonized, the entirety of a society), the post-1959 government sought to create more local resources for cultural production in order to give more people voices. A famous literacy campaign, new forms of educational access, and new publishing organizations did indeed affect a whole generation's experience of writing and support the emergence of local writers, as well as triggering greater interest in Latin American literature abroad.

As a young man Ángel Escobar benefited from these efforts: he received scholarships supporting his education, earned two degrees in the theater arts, and took an early interest in poetry. In 1977, he made his appearance on the national literary scene by winning the David Prize for emerging writers, awarded by Cuba's National Union of Artists and Writers (UNEAC) for his poetry collection *Viejas palabras de uso*. His 1985 collection, *Epílogo famoso*, then garnered another UNEAC prize, securing his place on the literary map.

Escobar's generation was taught throughout childhood to imagine itself working toward a utopian future. Critics Victor Fowler and Efraín Rodríguez Santana emphasize that many of Escobar's poems embrace the discourses of the island leaders and identify with the revolutionary project, particularly in his early work, where the lyric is less troubled. Fowler identifies displays of a historic vision supporting allegiance to the Revolution, as in this early moment when the speaker explicitly identifies with a "side" of history:

> . . . So okay, I'm on this side.
> If some scaffold collapses
> and I'm falling
> downward from my individual
> skeleton . . .
> . . . you can be sure that I'm falling from this side.

> [. . . Y bien, soy de este lado. / Si falla algún andamio / y caigo / de mi osamenta individual / abajo . . . / . . . sépase bien que caigo de este lado. ("XXVIII", de *Viejas palabras de uso*, 1978)]

The coherent identification with a particular "side" of history gives the speaker of the poem a community with which to identify, consistent with Roberto Férnandez Retamar's famous call to intellectual arms in the essay "Caliban": "To offend us they call us mambí, they call us black; but we reclaim as a mark of glory the honor of considering ourselves descendants of the mambí, descendants of the rebel, the runaway, independentista black—*never* descendants of the slaveholder. [. . .] To assume our condition as Caliban implies rethinking our history from the *other* side, from the *other* protagonist" (451–52). The choice of the *other* side provides a vocabulary for speaking about the perspectives of the downtrodden, who face hostility from forces both outside and inside themselves (such as the complex forces of colonization identified by Césaire in his *Discourse*). This pattern continues into Escobar's subsequent books.

Fowler also highlights the following excerpt from "Affabile," the opening poem of Escobar's 1984 *Allegro de sonata* (1984):

> Cuba yes,
> consequence of the sea,
> tendon, talon of sea,
> blade
> of
> dream.

Though the rooster may not sing
and
the barking of the dogs may throw me off.
Cuba yes.
Exceeding any return or prayer.

[Cuba sí, / resultado de mar, / tendón, talón de mar, / filo
/ de / sueño. / Aunque no cante el gallo / y / me sacuda el
ladrido de los perros. / Cuba sí. / Más que cualquier regreso
o cualquier ruego.]

The hope and affirmation in Escobar's poem, coupled with the nation's
status as a dream, complement other features of his early poetry that
establish an ethics linking the region's present to its past through revolu-
tionary discourse: speakers' claims to ancestry among slaves, identifica-
tion with fighters for Cuban national independence, and concerns about
a history of objectification and marginalization of peoples.

However, Fowler finds that over the course of his career Escobar
heightened the tensions around nation and writing, arriving at a deeply
agonic interplay between the two elements that locates him alongside
Raúl Hernández Novas and Carlos Alfonso, as the contemporary Cuban
poets who most explore dramatic conflicts involving nation and self. By
the late 1980s, a significant shift had complicated the identity and dis-
courses of the speaking selves in Escobar's poetry—the hallmarks of the
second stage of his career, reaffirmed by Puppo in subsequent studies.
By the time Escobar gets into *Breach of Trust*, alienation balloons. Hor-
ror saturates the poems, and playfulness bears a dark humor as well as
lines of escape. Hope and dream may allow for survival, granting range
to the abject lyric, but they do not cohere into a larger trajectory of social
progress toward utopia. Some of the factors driving this shift are seen
by Spanish-language critics to be collective, representative of Escobar's
society, a greater vision of violence in the modern world, and/or a philo-
sophical position. Other factors were profoundly personal yet are difficult
or impossible to disentangle from the articulation of social experience.

On the collective side are the discontents of Escobar's genera-
tion, which would be heightened by the island's disturbing transition
into the post-Soviet period, when the repetition of earlier revolutionary
discourses came to feel like gestures destined to remain incomplete.

Questions about the sufficiency of those discourses had begun to arise earlier in the 1980s, as the generation of children educated to live out the revolutionary future came of age. Many sought to push the island's leaders further toward affirming and achieving their stated revolutionary goals, as well as additional visions that could be implied in a liberatory mission, such as a fuller address to discrimination based on race, gender, and sexuality. At times this generation expressed frustration at seeing the same leaders hold sway from one decade into another, and another, and another; and they pushed their elders to recognize broader possibilities for revolutionary ethics and culture. The children of the revolution made internal criticisms of a Cuban society organized by their parents' generation, even as the Revolution exists for them as a historical fact that shaped their realities in often positive ways. In the 1980s they sought to create their own projects, debates, and visions for the future, a process that sometimes played into ambiguities in terms of who was thought to be working "inside" or "outside" of the revolutionary project.[5] Kicked off by the 1980 crisis associated with the exodus of some 125,000 Cubans who left the island in the Mariel Boatlift, this decade presented other major challenges to the expectations that had guided Escobar's generation to adulthood. And, regardless of their affiliations or confusions regarding specific social, political or cultural matters in earlier decades or the evolutions of the '80s, by 1989 Cubans had realized that they were all facing a strange new world.

The dismantling of the Soviet Union and its strategic alliances led to unforeseen, shattering changes to daily life in the 1990s. The island plunged into economic crisis as the support system of the Soviet Union fell away, while the US embargo continued to limit the development of alternative affiliations and resources. Access to basics like petroleum and foodstuffs became an ongoing, devastating challenge. This climate of change led to a new stage of debate in island society, one in which islanders were increasingly unable to imagine links between their austere daily lives and the utopian language earlier established to guide Cuban society.

Government platforms designed to intervene in historically oppressive structures and relations, aiming for example to reduce economic dependence on tourism, were compromised as islanders sought new forms of survival. Afro-Cubans reported a resurgence of racist treatment in the Havana area. With the resurfacing of structures from the past came undesired, ironic changes, such as pressures to accommodate ever more sexual tourism and permit the segregation of citizens around hotels, restaurants, beaches and other destinations frequented by tourists. Sectors with a record of post-revolutionary success, such as education and health care, remained points of pride but suffered from a spiraling lack of resources. Buildings around the city of Havana gained symbolic resonance for writers and photographers; despite some highly visible and successful renovations, a state of progressive ruination seemed more representative of the everyday experience of citizens.[6] Cuban poetry published in the 1990s is diverse, complex, and often a site for critical reflection about the challenges offered by the recent decades. For many writers, the new century looming on the horizon sharpened the need for new words, new phrases, and new images. In order to get to that next stage, they confronted the ruin of existing structures, both architectural and rhetorical.

Key to Fowler's overview of Escobar's oeuvre is his observation that by the late 1980s, the poetry became a site of testimony to pain, loss, and disaster. This blend is what Puppo identifies as the preeminence of lyric abjection, accompanying an outlook "now in clear dissidence with official voices" ("ya en clara disidencia con voces oficiales," 226).[7] One of the longer poems in *Breach of Trust*, "Punishment," reads to Fowler as "a powerful goodbye to the utopian thought that animated his first creations" ("un poderoso adiós al pensamiento utópico que animaba sus primeras creaciones," 123). The violence articulated in this poem "does not refer to an individual situation of a devastated self, but to a *we*. Its great shadow, its concern, is that of conserving ethical coherence to the end" ("no habla de la situación individual de un Yo desastrado, sino del nosotros. Su gran sombra, su preocupación, es la de conservar la coherencia ética hasta el fin," 123–24). Loudspeakers, pamphlets, and masks appear throughout the poem. These are accompanied by language that fails to signify reality for the speaker, so he experiences their theatricality as irony and violence. For Fowler, the "references to a crisis in the social fabric" could not be more striking ("las referencias a una crisis en el tejido social," 124). Seen in this light, Escobar's ability to capture social crisis becomes one of the most compelling elements of the book.

Escobar warns of looming dystopia, a reversal of tendencies to link islands—and the future of revolutionary Cuba—to utopia. Need the articulations of crisis and endangerment in *Breach of Trust* be understood primarily as dissent from Cuban leadership?

No: for his poems express varieties of alienation from the twentieth century as such—and thus from every society or state. "Escobar's writing places itself in the tradition of the 'No,'" states Francisco Morán, "but I hasten to add, in a sense that exceeds the Cuban political frame. Escobar's 'No' [. . .] would have been produced regardless of the Cuban Revolution, and in its most profound sense, it will endure in the Cuba to come after the Revolution" ("La escritura de Escobar se inserta en esa tradición del 'No,' pero—me apresuro a añadir—en un sentido que va más allá del marco politico cubano. El 'No' de Escobar [. . .] se habría producido igual sin la Revolución cubana, y en su significado más profundo, persistirá en 'la Cuba del día después'" [384]).

Expansions of time and space in *Breach of Trust* support Morán's perspective. The critique of the atom bomb in Escobar's prologue, "Broken mind," indicts the bomb's maker and by implication any state willing to adopt it as a tool of war. Poems such as "Punishment" and "Two chapters" would be hard to read in terms celebratory of (or even just consenting to) any government, any military, any surveillance system worldwide. Perhaps most illuminating is the tribute to Hatuey, "our incinerated brother," in Escobar's prologue. To fully grasp Escobar's remarks on the executed cacique, converted from man into thing, it helps to know that Cuban makers put his name on a brand of beer in the 1920s. This became very popular over the decades. (To see the "Indian's head" image of Hatuey used on vintage labels, just run a quick internet search.)

While *Breach of Trust* indicts the twentieth century, then, it is also illuminating to situate his critiques within a hemispheric frame taking a broader modernity into account, one dating back to the conquest of the Americas. Morán advocates for these broader frames of understanding, observing that Escobar's "No"

> does not accept the possibility of redemption, of a redeemer. This puts us on the road toward understanding the overwhelming expression of solitude, the sense of orphanhood, and his no less overstated hunger for love, which make of Escobar an open wound very similar to the continental wound that was César Vallejo. For both of them writing registers the cuts, wounds, failures to meet, chills, and solitudes that exceed any gesture of restoration or generosity, sincere as those may be. And it's not about a merely ontological

anguish—for there is indeed something of that—but instead about something that is also testimony, in both cases, to the marks left by history on indigenous and black skin.

[que no acepta la posibilidad de redención, de redentor. Esto podría ponernos en camino de comprender la sobrecogedora expresión de la soledad, el sentimiento de orfandad, y su no menos desmesurada hambre de amor, que hacen de Escobar una herida viva, muy similar a esa herida continental que fue César Vallejo. En uno y otro, la escritura registra cortes, heridas, desencuentros, escalofríos, soledades que están más allá de cualquier gesto reparador o de generosidad por sinceros que éstos sean. Y no se trata de una angustia meramente ontológica—si bien hay algo de esto—sino que es el testimonio también, en ambos casos, de las marcas dejadas por la historia en la piel del indígena y del negro. (384–85)]

Consistent with Morán's scholarly overview, which highlights the broadest social, historical and poetic forces dislodging the self from itself—Escobar's Latin American take on *I is someone else*—is the poetic representation of Escobar by his dear friend, sometime lover, and fellow writer Soleida Ríos.

Ríos, who met with me in Havana in 2013 to discuss a poem she wrote about him, identifies with Escobar on many levels. She too combines the city with the country in her body of work: like him, Ríos was born into humble circumstances in Oriente and migrated to the Havana area, where she developed connections with fellow writers around the city as an adult. Seven years older than Escobar, she remembers that she once *thought* they had first met in Havana after she admired his first book of published poetry (*Viejas palabras de uso*, the book that appeared in 1978). It was not until she and Escobar had been friends for many years that he confessed to having seen her many years earlier, back in eastern Cuba. There Ríos read her poetry at a public event. Escobar, then a teenager, was in the audience. Her work impressed him. It was not only the quality of her writing that he liked, as he later told Ríos; he was surprised to hear how she worked with her own origins in eastern Cuba, because

he had worried that his own similar origins were unworthy to be poetic material. After listening to her read on that fateful day, Escobar told Ríos, he went back to work on an unfinished manuscript. It was none other than an early draft of *Viejas palabras de uso*, the very book that led to their meeting and friendship in Havana. Ríos and Escobar remained friends, and occasional lovers, for the rest of his life. As the above anecdote indicates, their poetic affiliation was always at the heart of this relationship. After Escobar's suicide Ríos could not write about him for many years, but she eventually produced a set of poems mourning his loss.

In her striking elegy "Ángel Éscobar: Excogitate *The Wheel*," Ríos emphasizes the poet's sensuality, setting it against layers of tension. She explores his battle with schizophrenia in tight relation to poetry (represented in her poem by the canonical figure of Lezama) and the legacy of racial and imperial violence that shaped the Spanish language itself. This violence, a linguistic facet of thingification, bleeds into Cuban literary legacies. In her poem Escobar's existence is synonymous with his battle for cultural legitimacy.

> *He sees a black man rise up, one all full of hair*
> Red robe, black inkwell.
> *He opens the book, re-examines that which comes and that*
> *which goes . . .*
> Excogitates. Then becomes an emptied site
> (ñinga!)
> because in the Royal Academy's dictionary
> LO NEGRO the BLACK THING,
> BLACK THING gets in the way.
> Even today.

> [*Se ve ascender un hombre negro, está lleno de pelos* / Manto rojo, tintero negro. / *Abre el libro, repasa lo que llega y lo que se va...*/ Excogita. Luego deviene sitio solitario / (¡ñinga!) / porque en el Diccionario de la Lengua / LO NEGRO es torba. /Todavía. (100–7)]

The exclamation "Nínga!" could be translated as "just a jot"—a dual assertion in which the non-Spanish exclamation performs the existence

of a diasporic other (for readers who are conscious of African diasporic presences in the Caribbean), but one potentially undercut by the message of insignificance about his mark/speech (perceived, hegemonically, as no more than a jot). While Ríos refers obliquely to Escobar's illness and one of his unsuccessful suicide attempts in this poem, she also suggests that his individual pain be seen as a symptom of the historical oppression of the peoples of African diaspora, across centuries:

> I revolve (ruptured) between sky and earth.

> Yes. An elliptical hole would open my head in two.
> Cables, chains ran through. The chains.
> *Écubier.*
> Pretty blacks in the slave quarter.
> Haitians in the workers' quarter.
> Jacobo, Juliana, Francisco, Ta José.
> Sometimes I fall face down.
> Oh, Mother.
> I tried to drink the dew
> like a wildflower.

> [Ruedo (roto) entre cielo y tierra. / / Sí. Un agujero elíptico abría en dos mi cabeza. / Pasaban cables, cadenas. Las cadenas. / *Écubier.* / Negros lindos del barracón. / Haitianos del barracón. / Jacobo, Juliana, / Francisco, Ta José. / A veces caigo boca abajo. / Ay, Madre. / Quise abrevar en el rocío / como una flor silvestre. (109–20)]

The speaker's abject position evokes the way in which race remains a fraught subject in Cuba, with tensions threaded throughout contemporary uses of language. Jafiri Allen observes, "The revolution inarguably improved the relative position of black Cubans. [. . .] Also inarguable, however, is that *even a revolution* has yet to undo the centuries of racist and sexist hegemony that have shaped the nation" (61–62). As Ríos suggests in her elegy, the weight of history acts on everyday language to further trauma even when speakers hope their society has overcome it: "Still unacknowledged [. . .] are the ways in which racism and sexism undergird rhetorics and policies of racelessness" that permeate everyday life (Allen 62).

Like Ríos, I find that many poets who knew Escobar and read his poems as they first emerged take pains to put his cultural critiques and aesthetics of abjection into a particular context. I eventually realized that this context is essential to presenting Escobar in English for the first time, particularly because the book is *Breach of Trust*, with its poetics of dissent. So far everyone who has brought up the topic with me has found it essential to complicate his/her sense of that dissent. They state that had he lived into the new century, Escobar would never have left Cuba—in spite of his critiques of stagnant rhetoric in the Special Period, his expressions of alienation highlighted by Morán and others, and even some stray opinions from fellow writers that his poetry can be seen as an indictment of a surveillance culture pervading the island's everyday life. These affirmations that Escobar would never have left the island and its society behind do not depend on whether their sources remain in Cuba today or have left to build a life elsewhere (which many islanders, including many writers who knew Escobar, did as the post-Soviet economic crisis continued to deepen). People told me that Escobar spoke of a lingering sense of loyalty to the revolutionary project writ large, despite his irony and critical vision, and he felt committed to participation in his national and local communities. His widow, writers who are his contemporaries, and members of a younger generation strongly influenced by his poetry all said that Escobar felt compelled to recognize the importance of the revolution's crucial, albeit human and flawed, historical existence. For example, a Cuban poet who is now quite happy to be living in Spain shared his memory that one of Escobar's jobs involved working with young people who benefited from governmental scholarships similar to the ones he himself had received. Escobar spoke of how he valued that service work very deeply, and it gave him an important sense of identification with ongoing island social programs.[8]

Despite the marked abject stance of Escobar's poetry and its profound commitment to dissent, then, I do not describe him as a "dissident" writer. It seems to me that when this word is tossed around in English (and outside the island) it rapidly loses its complexity. Instead it will be more useful for future studies of Escobar's literary legacy to explore contexts like "re-globalization," as briefly sketched by Allen: "The vexed homecoming of global capital to Cuba—which I want to call re-globalization—has brought material hardship and existential quandary to the country. For blacks, and non-heteronormative individuals, 'deviant' and political possibilities expanded during Cuba's Special Period in Time of Peace" (3–4). Escobar's poetic abjection, voiced by self-identified scapegoats, unfurls under these conditions.

To my mind the very richness of this conversation is the main point. Escobar's poems come to figure as testimony not only to pain, loss, alienation, disaster, and the threat of a final fall but also to love, survival, creativity, and flight: a life fully imbricated in the textures of a contradictory, changing world. Cubans have not remained frozen in time since the Revolution took place, as so many tourism guides suggest with their colorful photos of cars preserved since the 1950s. Cuba is a complex society. It underwent profound changes during Escobar's lifetime and continues to change in the new century. As the people who knew him struggled to account for the many issues and feelings in play in our conversations, they often paused, then declared Escobar to be the voice of an entire generation.

A Tale of Several Cities

Escobar's generation witnessed more than the unfolding of new historical conditions within Cuba. In *Breach of Trust* Escobar evokes state violence specific to the late 1960s and the 1970s in other parts of Latin America, particularly the Southern Cone. Tanks and soldiers figure in his poems, while prisons and cruel ceremonies become poetic emblems of assault on the human body and mind. Focusing on the role of Chilean imagery in *Breach of Trust* is essential step toward understanding how Escobar's transnational critique of modern states cuts across deep political divisions.

When drafting my preliminary translation of "Notes toward a biography of Helene Zarour," I knew that the poem evoked recent Chilean history: even if its climate hadn't awakened memories from my own conversations with people there decades ago, the poem's two main characters and their ambiguous, ominous setting refer to people and events in Chile in the years following the 1973 military coup that removed President Salvador Allende from power. General Augusto Pinochet rose to power in the aftermath of the coup and set about putting an end to Allende's socialist reforms. During the seventeen years of his dictatorship, Pinochet forwarded a neoliberal economy in Chile, privatizing resources and promoting exports. Proposing to reclaim the nation from the perceived disorder that had overtaken Chilean society under Allende's government, Pinochet's regime oversaw the detention, torture, and disappearance of thousands of people as a means of returning "order" to society.

Helene Zarour, who would become the title character in Esco-
bar's poem, was in real life a member of MIR, a leftist organization per-
ceived as undesirable by Pinochet's government. She was captured as a
political prisoner in the mid-1970s and held at Villa Grimaldi, a large res-
idence on the outskirts of Santiago that had been converted into a prison.
Profoundly traumatized by her experience there, Zarour was eventually
released but went on to commit suicide.[9]

Arturo Romo Mena, the guard whom Escobar names in this
same poem, is infamous in Chile and beyond for his role in the sexual
torture that took place at Villa Grimaldi. Leigh Payne, the author of a
study about truth commissions in the late twentieth century, writes that
Romo became a "personification of terror" for Chilean survivors of the
prison at Villa Grimaldi (109). When they later sought justice, many
mentioned him by name:

> The Chilean Truth Commission considered no fewer than
> eighty accusations of rape and other forms of torture by
> Romo during his two years (1973-1975) as a civilian mem-
> ber of the dictatorship's secret military-police unit, DINA.
> Because of Romo's particular role in DINA and his personal
> style, victims and survivors were able to identify him after
> the end of the dictatorship. (Payne 107)

Interviewed about his work in 1995 for the salacious television show
Primer Impacto, Romo appeared in a dirty t-shirt and made contradic-
tory statements alternating among pride, justification, and denial of his
actions. He characterized torture and disappearance as essential tools of
battle on behalf of a noble cause: the restoration of order in a nation bat-
tling the evils of international communism. During his strange televised
"confession," broadcast by Univisión out of Miami and across Latin Amer-
ica, Romo would have known that he didn't have the immunity from pros-
ecution that had been extended to members of the military in Chile; his
remarks were somewhat guarded. However, he appeared to want to claim
credit and respect for his work at Villa Grimaldi.[10] He denied actually tor-
turing anyone, demonstrating indignation at accusations. But he under-
cut these denials within the interview by indicating that he did not define
activities such as electrical shock as torture. He displayed sadistic pleasure

when describing (with hand gestures) wetting women's bodies, applying electrodes to their nipples, and turning on the power (Payne 109).

Escobar's poem captures the haze of Zarour's repeated violation by Romo and others at Villa Grimaldi and foregrounds the ambiguous boundaries between trauma and its representations. What I did not initially know when I first translated this poem was how very personal the connection was that motivated Escobar to write his poem. After my translation was accepted for publication by *The Brooklyn Rail/InTranslation*, Ana María Jiménez sent me her own story about the original poem.

In 1983 Escobar met Jiménez, who would become his second wife. She had survived years of imprisonment in the mid-1970s at Villa Grimaldi—alongside Helene Zarour. She has bitter memories of Romo and the abuse the women suffered as captives. After her release from Villa Grimaldi, Jiménez saw no option but to leave Chile: her freedom was too tenuous, the climate too dangerous. She sought asylum in various nations (including the United States, which refused) and found it in Cuba. There, Jiménez and Escobar fell in love.

They bonded through joyful activity, such as the music they played together, but also through their painful discussions of trauma and survival. Escobar began composing much of the poetry in *Abuso de confianza* between 1983 and 1986, their first few years together. When Jiménez was able to visit to her country many years later, Escobar accompanied her to Chile with an invitation and the assistance of a writing fellowship. The first edition of Escobar's book, containing the poem drawn from their conversations about her experience at Villa Grimaldi, was published in Chile in 1992. *Abuso de confianza* was subsequently reprinted in Cuba.

Escobar's "Notes toward a biography of Helene Zarour" is a passionate indictment of the structural violence that tore through Latin American societies in the second half of the twentieth century.[11] The poem identifies violence as one of the key forces haunting the book as a whole, and it links Escobar's work to other contemporary poetry investigating trauma born of political imprisonment, torture, and assassinations. For example, Chilean poet Raúl Zurita's meditations on "The Fields of Delirium" and the "Plains of Pain," on faces smashed into mirrors, on the confused and spiraling "madness of the madness of the madness of the . . ." (. . . *what?*), similarly adopt poetry as a space for grappling with effects of state violence too traumatic to be fully named in writing (17, 83, 85).

Examination : Auscultation

The wounded selves in *Breach of Trust* do not necessarily expire. Jiménez has shared concerns about obscuring her husband's gift for articulating life and beauty when commentators focus exclusively on the painful elements of the work, particularly his illness and eventual suicide (Lynd 127). In this book the representation of trauma caused by torture is additionally compelling, so it may be all the more important to listen to her point about losing sight of affirmations. A fuller reading of Escobar's abject poetry can locate its life at the points of confrontation between a most vital energy and its moments of exhaustion.

A patient's rage while subjected to analytical probing and diagnosis emerges in "Hospitals," "Funny Papers," and especially in "Guests." Words that scrutinize, administer, and discipline weave through the poems. And so language used to classify health and illness becomes a target: something to be resisted, disrupted with dark humor. This feature of *Breach of Trust* makes it a useful introduction to poems appearing in Escobar's other books. For example, in "Protection of the order," a poem from the collection *Cuando salí de la Habana*, he also incorporates several lines expressing resistance to an analytical gaze that turns the self into a thing to be viewed and diagnosed. Escobar first found the lines in a poem by Jean-Michel Basquiat. Other moments in this poem also suggest suspicion toward psychoanalytic and literary analyses:

> If one adds a detail to reality
> one transforms the world. Méliès did it—
> and ended up selling toys in a fair.
> I'm not Basquiat (1960-1988) but I will raise my voice—
> you all can tell me to go to hell,
> I'll tell you like he did: "This examination is over."
> I don't have what it takes, according to Hölderlin, for
> the golden mediocrity of life. I think I think, with him,
> that what lasts is made by poets—and so like Franz
> I have a curious animal, half kitty,
> half lamb—inheritance from the father. Franz
> comes to be the poet, and I dig another tunnel of the Twenty.
> I am an old corrupt mole; I go back to the ark—
> while Voltaire tends his own garden. And I say:

I'd like to carry out an act liberating me as it unfolds—
but the thing internal to what is called an act, is the fact that
one does not know oneself, says Jacques Lacan my
psychoanalyst to me.
The desire to live in more than one world doesn't give
me salvation—
I don't know Blumenberg, I'm not lost in the forest
like a maiden. Or yes: I am lost, and alone, an animal
quartered before so many roads: they break it open,
knock it over.
Then he tells me about Sunday's reading
which says mean-ing is the re-nun-ci-a-tion of a mean-ing.
I'm scared,
but *tomorrow I'm off to Sibanicú, tomorrow.*[12]

[Si se le agrega un detalle a la realidad / se transforma al
mundo. Méliès lo hizo—/ y terminó vendiendo juguetes en
una feria. / Yo no soy Basquiat (1960-1988), pero alzaré la
voz—/ ustedes podrían igual decirme que vaya al diablo, /
yo les diré como él: "El examen ha terminado". / No tengo
lo que se requiere para, según Hölderlin, / la dorada medi-
ocridad de la vida. Creo creer, con él, / que lo que queda
lo fundan los poetas—así tengo, / como Franz, un animal
curioso, mitad gatito, / mitad cordero—es una herencia del
padre. Franz / viene a ser el poeta, y yo cavo otro túnel del
Veinte. / Yo soy un viejo topo corrupto; vuelvo al arca—/
mientras Voltaire cultiva su jardín propio. Y digo: / Quisiera
hacer un acto que me libere andando—pero / lo interno a lo
que se llama acto, es que se desconoce / a sí mismo, me dice
Jacques Lacan, mi sicoanalista. / No me salva el querer que
vivamos en más de un mundo—/ no conozco a Blumen-
berg, ni estoy perdido en el bosque / como una doncella.
O sí: estoy perdido, y solo, res / destazada ante tantos cami-
nos: la desjarretan, la tumban. / Luego me dice rintintín de
la lectura de domingo / que el sentido es la renuncia a un
sentido. Tengo miedo, / pero mañana me voy p'a Sibanicú,
mañana. ("Resguardo del orden")]

The concluding line is taken from a popular Cuban song, suggesting the speaker's playful method of escape from the analytical gaze. The strategy of exiting via a playful evasion also reappears in *Breach of Trust*, most obviously at the end of "Funny papers." Escobar recycles a line from a memory recorded by William Blake to open this escape route: "Can you not make me truly insane?" (Davis 99).

As medicine takes the measure of the human body, it is not exclusively an oppressive force. Listening carefully to the body is also a method for confirming life. While translating poems from *Breach of Trust* and other books, I've been struck by Escobar's use of the verb *auscultar*. He uses it in "Another text about another proof and another proof," the poem with which he engages Lezama and the issue of raising one's voice to join the canonical literary dialogue. *Auscultar* can simply refer to sounding something out, and it could be translated in more everyday English without losing a sense of Escobar's tone. Yet it is also a specialized medical term, "to auscultate," and that medical register is equally evocative in translation. It is "the action of listening to sounds from the heart, lungs, or other organs, typically with a stethoscope, as a part of medical diagnosis" (OED). The speaker of "Another text about another proof and another proof" suggestively pauses to take his own measure at the poem's halfway point. Auscultation follows immediately after his evocations of nothingness, suggesting that the poem is proof of something surviving negation.

Breach of Trust itself, outliving its author, represents the spirit of survival to many Spanish-language readers. Appeals for justice and love, implicit as well as explicit, are essential components of its abject theatricality. It is my hope that in all its pain and difficulty—precisely *because* of Escobar's compelling, painful drive to confront thingification face to (non)face—the English translation succeeds in delivering this spirit.

Kristin Dykstra

Endnotes

1. I could have chosen to translate Escobar's highlighted term, "conveniencia," as "convenience" instead of "advisability." I prefer "advisability" as a more flexible and ideologically loaded term. Whereas "convenience" invokes a decision in the moment about what seems easiest to do, a forgettable instant, "advisibility" suggests more extended reflection or pressure about how one ought to make decisions. In a decision-making process commonly invoked sources are "common sense" or "rational" explanation. Therefore, the individual intersects with society and authority when contemplating the advisable course of action. And so one moves, in Escobar's prologue, into and out of twisted ideas used to rationalize creations like the atom bomb.

2. For the complete essay on Escobar by Marqués, in English translation, see *Jacket* 38: http://jacketmagazine.com/38/escobar-about.shtml. For another by Rodríguez, also in my translation, see "Angel Escobar and the other shipwrecks," in *Sirena: Poetry, Art, and Criticism* (2010) 2: 122–25.

3. Other references in the book involve Escobar's contemporaries, generating a different register of intertextuality to be explored in future research. For example, after Escobar's death, Efraín Rodríguez Santana published a novel in which the protagonist is Escobar. His fictional Escobar explains that the name Oersman (from the poem in *Breach of Trust*, "Oersman's novel") is a coded reference to Efraín Rodríguez Santana himself. The fictional character Escobar explains that he began with the letter O, added ERS from his friend's initials, and tacked on "Man" at the end.

4. See this and other memories from Villalobo in "Quick Now" and "Recitations." *Jacket2* ("Intermedium" commentary series), 2015. Digital: http://jacket2.org/commentary/quick-now and http://jacket2.org/commentary/recitations.

5. This ambiguous terminology characterizing the rights of writers and artists was institutionalized with Fidel Castro's 1961 pamphlet "Palabras a los intelectuales" ("Words to the Intellectuals").

6. Two excellent collections for more context about post-1989 Cuba, including observations about cultural expression, are *Havana Beyond the Ruins: Cultural Mappings after 1989* (ed. Anke Birkenmaier and Esther Whitfield, Durham: Duke UP, 2011) and *Cuba in the Special Period: Culture and Ideology in the 1990s* (Ariana Hernández Reguant, Ariana, NY: Palgrave MacMillan, 2009).

7. Puppo situates José Kozer as another important voice of Cuba's lyric abject poetry in this decade, preceding Escobar and emphasizing a state of existence without a nation ("sin nación").

8. Juliet Lynd has written an essay based on her interview with his widow; it explores related issues in more detail.

9. Ernesto Guajardo's article about Escobar, published by a Chilean venue, includes many of the details I note here and serves as evidence of transnational visibility for Escobar's poem.

10. Payne speculates that Romo was overconfident that his declarations would receive a positive reception because the reporters were Cubans based in Miami—he may have assumed that they sympathized with his brand of politics and would make an effort to present him in a good light, which they did not.

11. See Lynd for a useful and more extensive discussion of this topic.

12. Translation previously published in *Sibila-English*, 2010. I have not emphasized race or visual art as subject matter here because medical examination is the focus of this segment, but Escobar's works are fascinating in terms of both topics. There are also suggestive class overtones in his segue from intellectual culture into popular music at the close of this poem.

Works Cited

Aguilera, Carlos A. "Funny papers. Apuntes sobre la poesía de Ángel Escobar." In *Rodríguez Santana*, 2001, 145–49.

Allen, Jafari S. *¡Venceremos? The Erotics of Black Self-Making in Cuba*. Durham: Duke UP, 2011.

"Auscultation, *noun*." *The Oxford Dictionary of English* (revised edition). Ed. Catherine Soanes and Angus Stevenson. Oxford University Press, 2005. *Oxford Reference Online*. Oxford University Press: Illinois State University (May 15, 2010). http://www.oxfordreference.com/views/ENTRY.html?subview=Main&entry=t140.e4619

Césaire, Aimé. *Discourse on Colonialism* (*Discours sur le colonialisme*, 1950). Revised and expanded. Trans. Joan Pinkham. New York: Monthly Review Press, 1972, 2000.

Davis, Michael. *William Blake: A New Kind of Man*. Berkeley and Los Angeles: University of California Press, 1977.

Escobar, Ángel. *Abuso de confianza*. Santiago de Chile: Kipus 21 Editora, 1992.

———. *Ángel Escobar: Poesía completa*. Ed. Jesús David Curbelo and Misael Verdazco. Havana: Ediciones UNIÓN, 2006.

Esteban, Angel, and Álvaro Salvador. *Antología de la poesía cubana*. IV: 20th Century. Madrid: Editorial Verbum, 2002.

Fowler, Victor. "El muro anterior a toda pérdida." In Rodríguez Santana 2001, 109–31.

González Echevarría, Roberto. "José Martí: An Introduction." In *José Martí: Selected Writings*.

Guajardo, Ernesto. "El poeta como un espejo: Ángel Escobar en Chile." *Letras s5.com: Página chilena al servicio de la cultura*, Proyecto Patrimonio (2007). http://www.letras.s5.com/eg241207.html

Heller, Ben. *Assimilation/Generation/Resurrection: Contrapuntal Readings in the Poetry of José Lezama Lima*. Lewisburg, Pennsylvania: Bucknell University Press, 1997.

Lezama Lima, José. *José Lezama Lima: Selections*. Ed. Ernesto Livon-Grosman. Berkeley and Los Angeles: University of California Press, 2005.

Lynd, Juliet. "Reflections on a Conversation with Ana María Jiménez, Wife of Ángel Escobar." *Sirena: Poesía, arte y crítica* (2010.2): 126–36.

Marqués de Armas, Pedro. "Gran salto hacia fuera." In Rodríguez Santana 2001, 139–44.

Martí, José. Ed. and trans. Esther Allen. *José Martí: Selected Writings*. New York: Penguin, 2002.

Martín Hernández, Evelyne. "En el umbral de la sombra." In Rodríguez Santana 2001, 48–55.

Morán, Francisco. "Ángel Escobar: La luz sobre el asfalto." *Mandorla: New Writing from the Americas/Nueva escritura de las Américas* 11 (2008): 382–98.

Payne, Leigh A. *Unsettling Accounts: Neither Truth Nor Reconciliation in Confessions of State Violence*. Durham, North Carolina: Duke University Press, 2008.

Puppo, María Lucía. "Apuntes de 'La ciudad podrida': la configuración distópica de La Habana en la poesía de Ángel Escobar." *Estudios Caribeños/Caribbean Studies* 39.1–2 (January–December 2011): 223–39.

Rimbaud, Arthur. *Rimbaud Complete*. Vol. 1: Poetry and Prose. Ed., trans., and int. Wyatt Mason. New York: The Modern Library, 2003.

Ríos, Soleida. "Ángel Escobar: Excogitate *The Wheel*" ("Angel Escobar: Excogitar *La Rueda*," from *Secadero* [Havana: Ediciones UNIÓN, 2009]; also published in *Escritos al revés* [Havana: Letras Cubanas, 2009]). Trans. Kristin Dykstra. *Eleven Eleven: Journal of Literature and Art* 15 (2013).

———. Conversation with Kristin Dykstra. Home of Soleida Ríos. Havana, Cuba, January 7, 2013.

Rodríguez Santana, Efraín. "Ángel Escobar y los otros náufragos." In Escobar 2006. 438–42.

———, ed. *Ángel Escobar: El escogido*. Havana: Ediciones UNIÓN, 2001.

———, ed. and int. *Fatiga ser dos sombras (Antología poética)*. Madrid: Editorial Betanía, 2002.

Salgado, César Augusto. "Hybridity in New World Baroque Theory." *Journal of American Folklore*, 112.445 (1999): 316–31. *Humanities Source*.

Zurita, Raúl. *Purgatory: A Bilingual Edition* (*Purgatorio*, 1979). Trans. Anna Deeny. Berkeley and Los Angeles: Unversity of California Press, 2009.

Breach of Trust / Abuso de Confianza

Portrait of Ángel Escobar by Nelson Villalobo taken in 1987 at Villalobo's home and studio in Virgen del Camino. Located in San Miguel del Padrón, this area is one of the fifteen municipalities that make up the province of Havana.

Mente rota

Antes de que alguien (¿*all*, quién?) lea, participe, de unos textos que suscribe Nadie,[1] Otro (¡oh potros?) los ("cataclismo de dialogo") hablará ante ustedes (¿huy, *tendresse*?); pero, y aun sin peros, en primer lugar (¿un abandono?) les presentará a un amigo (no hay otros lugares) que les ofrecerá a un conocido (¿cono, sí, no?) que a su vez (¿ves?) les (¿*leave me down*?) entregará (¿entre, car, ra, ra, ra?) a otro (¡oh, potros!) como víctima Propiciatoria: él, rosa, Buda, llama, desrealizará su tartaleo. Escuchen. Hay, además, uno (¿de, más?) que espera, y desespera, porque no le traiga el tartaleo prebendas ni castigos.

Todos son invisibles y, en sí mismos, han perdido los sentidos: anhelan cumplir dos impulsos: el de un espíritu y otro de Non Nata. (El espíritu, a más no ponerse el sombrero, Non Nata, por si no es evidente, es *non nata*, es desconocida.)

Todos, los invisibles sin sentidos, han entrado al idioma por las escaleras de servicio. Incluso viendo las jarchas y a Jehuda Ha Levi (1075–140?): "Enfermo está: ¿cuándo sanará?", o no viéndolos. Dicen que dicen que escribió Aristóteles: "Ir en busca de una explicación y admirarse, es reconocer que se ignora". Les place, angustia, este ignorar, este desaprendizaje remoto en su cercanía flagrante. El indio, aquel realmente él, se dejó (no tenía alternativas, nadie las tiene) quemar en la hoguera, prefiriendo terminar en sí. Para no aprender: no razono con la razón razonable de lo otro, de los otros. Hoy vuelve a la mudez suya y de su perro el indio, mudez que habla. La apabullante trivialización del ser lo ha convertido en una cerveza. El no saber sapiente del *simple* lo ha transmutado: es el sol siendo él: helo ahí, fijo, lo que, yuxtapuesto, es fue y será, también, un anhelo de Da Vinci: *il sole non se muove*.

Aparece Da Vinci, no para prestigiar este argumento sino porque más bien lo desampara: "Él deseaba con seguridad hacerse un maestro en la imitación de la naturaleza y enseñar el camino a los demás", según Freud, y el *simple* del que no se habla no tiene deseo ni seguridad: está expuesto en, por y para la naturaleza, que se ha convertido en sociedad, y su no deseo, su inseguridad lo catapultan hacia la desenseñanza: *el camino*, él sabe, no sabe, se ha convertido en "conveniencia"; *los demás* esperan que sean todos y todo practicables, viables, funcionales. Hatuey, la botella o la lata, lo es; Hatuey ese aluvión de nada, todo, esa carga de mudez, grito, entre el sol, y el incinerado carnal, no.

2

Broken mind

Before anyone (*many*, one?) reads, takes part in, writings to which No One subscribes,[1] An Other (uh, Cover?) will voice them (in "utter cataclysm") to all you present (ahhh, *tendresse?*); but, and even without buts, in the first place (an abandon?) he will introduce you to a friend (there are no other places) who will offer you a *cognoscente* (cog: nay, assent?) who in turn (have you learned?) will (won't *get me down?*) turn it over (in a car are, are, are?) to another (ahhhh brother!) as Scapegoat: rose, Buddha, flame, he will cancel out his stammering. Listen. There's also somebody (or else) who gives it time, and gives it up, for the stammering gives way to no sinecure or punishment.

All are invisible and have lost their senses in their own right: they want to give in to two impulses: one of a spirit, and another of Non Nata. (The spirit until it can't go on being spirited anymore; Non Nata, in case this isn't already obvious, is *non nata*, unknown.)

All of them, these invisible senseless figures, entered the language through its service door. Even seeing the *kharjas* and Yehuda Halevi (1075–140?): "It is ill: when will it be cured?"—or not seeing them. They say that they say that Aristotle wrote, "To go in search of an explanation and wonder, is to recognize that one is ignorant." It pleases them, anguish, this ignoring, unlearning distance in its flagrant proximity. Hatuey the Indian, that faraway presence most truly himself, allowed himself (he had no alternative, no one does) to burn at the stake, preferring termination. In order not to learn: I don't reason with the reasonable reason of the other, the other ones. Today the Indian returns to his mute silence and to that of his dog, a muteness that speaks. The shattering trivialization of Hatuey's existence has turned him into a brand of beer. The state of not knowing oneself aware of the *simplest thing* has transmuted him: being himself, he is the sun: I have it here at hand, stable, something that when juxtaposed is, was and will be, a dream Da Vinci dreamed too: *il sole non si muove*.

Da Vinci appears here not in order to lend prestige to this storyline, but because he abandons it: "He certainly wanted to become a master imitator of nature and to show the way to others," according to Freud, and the *simplest thing* which goes unspoken holds neither desire nor certainty: is exposed in, by, and for nature; which has turned into society, and his non-desire, his insecurity catapults him toward

El siglo XX lo ha sacrificado todo al funcionalismo; ha deslegitimado el *quién* y el *algo* ante la función. No es esto, justamente hablando, único, suyo, de él, coto privado a/de su feroz realeza, pero en él llega al extremo aberrante, al límite intolerable para la conciencia, que se aliena o juega, no alcanza fijeza; se intenta, no ella, sino todos y todo contra ella, construir y reconstruir, construir y reconstruir, en cambio, como un objeto de "perención incorporada", "para una eternidad razonable", la obligación y el castigo y en cuya permisible medida "la belleza se da como *algo más*, por añadidura, (y) es un acontecimiento suplementario, un epifenómeno". A.A. Moles y E. Wahl nos dicen que "en la práctica, esto significa lucha contra la inutilidad, censura y rigor; el funcionalismo es, en sí, *ascético*".

Cuando el sol del trópico, en su esplendor, se hace sobre la piel y el alma, el que viene, visitante, entra y, como al desgaire, mienta al indio, que así renace (o no) en la modestia última del trato. Esto, para la *función*, es inútil, censurable y nada riguroso.

¿Cómo entrar el cuándo, y todas las posibles preguntas, de/a una palabra, un gesto, una actitud, una intención, una frase, una línea de verso que intentan, intentaran o intentarán, un accidente, una falla, lo no aconsejable, y el hacer, predicado de sí mismo, hacer hace, que se fijen contra el escarceo de los gustos gustables, y digan *no*, entendida esa palabra como señal hierática del signo, a la moneda que en el bolsillo, o en el pecho, coloca la usura de la eficacia predicha y programada y ya convertida en distopía?

Hay (o no) testimonios y posibles respuestas de ello: para Unamuno, que vivió entre el siglo anterior y este, "toda conciencia es conciencia del dolor", y creo que a su dolor no le dolió como le duele en su evidencia a Nadie, la cosificación que impuesta ronda, ejercida incita (la conciencia hoy es objeto que entra en los cambios oscilantes del valor): habría acrecentado su *sentimiento trágico de la vida*. Valéry: *il n'est rien de si beau que ce qui n'existe pas*: fue su ventura; para el *Nouveau Petit Larousse* que, a su pensar, lo retrotrae a la reconciliación con el medio *il commence par publier des poèmes, mais voit dans la litterature une dangereuse idolatrie*: oponiéndo un *pero*, acusando un *peligro*. Para conjurar ambos lo llevaron vivo al aula, a la academia: Valéry escucho una (antologable) *mise en scène*, una función de su *Cimetière Marine*: lejos queda su disfunción. ¿Dónde?

unlearning: he knows, doesn't know, *the way*, has turned into "advisability"; *the rest of them* hope that everyone and everything may be practicable, viable, functional. Hatuey, the bottle or can of beer, is just that; Hatuey the alluvium left behind by nothing, by everything, that charge of muteness, shouting, between the sun and our incinerated brother, no.

The XX century has sacrificed everything to functionalism, has delegitimized the *who* and the *something* in deference to function. Strictly speaking this isn't unique to the century, isn't a special preserve deprived of/for its cruel magnificence. But in the twentieth century functionalism arrives at its aberrant extreme, the intolerable limit of consciousness, which alienates or makes its plays. It achieves no stability, which is not its aim, but anything and everything at odds with it, to construct and reconstruct, construct and reconstruct, by contrast, as an object of "statute of limitation," "for a reasonable eternity," liability and punishment, and within its permissible measure beauty occurs "as *something extra*, additive, (and) is a supplementary occasion, an epiphenomenon." A.A. Moles and E. Wahl tell us that "in practice, this means a battle against uselessness, it means censorship and rigor; functionalism is, in and of itself, *ascetic.*"

When the tropical sun in all its splendor falls on the skin and soul, a person arrives, a visitor, enters and almost with a certain contempt, drops Hatuey's name; then the Indian is rebirthed (or not) into the latest trappings of the deal. This, according to the view of *function*, is useless, censurable, and not at all rigorous.

How do you approach the *when*; and all the possible questions concerning or posed by a word, gesture, attitude, intention, phrase, line of verse; which attempt, might attempt, or may well attempt an accident, a failure, something inadvisable; and with making predicated upon itself, making make? How do you set words against the digression of pleasures capable of giving pleasure, and make them say *no*—a word understood as hieratic signal of the sign—to the mark, the currency, which in your pocket or close to your heart acquires the usury of predetermined and pre-programmed efficacy, already converted into dystopia?

There are (or aren't) testimonials and potential responses: for Unamuno, who lived between the prior century and this one, "all consciousness is consciousness of pain," and I don't think his pain pained him as much as Nobody is pained by his proof, the thingification which

Para no hacer largo ni demasiado eficaz este maldito enigma (?) perorado se mientan dos nombres: Dadá, Duchamp: el segundo, que lleva al primero, se eriza el 2 de noviembre de 1962: "les arrojé a la cabeza los porta-botellas y el urinario como una provocación, y ahora resulta que admiran su belleza estética". Pero *ese* admirarse, *ese* asombro, no es "un reconocer que se ignora", es una mediatización, es "una reconciliación del ser humano conservador con el arte subversivo". (Moles, Wahl), es el *kitsch* que "siempre está en proceso de evadirse hacia la racionalidad" (Hermann Broch). *Belleza, estética* como accesorios del ascetismo y del hedonismo (donde es posible por abundancia) de la función.

No sé si Duchamp al hacer su "caja verde" conocía el *Ne lui riblen sa Cage vert* (*Le Testament*, CXX, sexto verso) de Villon (1431-1463) que Carlos Alvar traduce *no le quiten su cajita verde*, y hace notar que *cage vert* para Thuasne, es una metáfora que "equivale a una mujer de vida licenciosa". Villon pide que *Detusca et ses gendarmes*, no se la quiten, no se la roben *a frère Baude*: no sólo la *cage vert*, Detusca y sus hombres se lo han robado todo a Balde, a Villon, a Duchamp y a ti.

En la Edad Media, en lugar del número, se colocaban insignias en las puertas de las casas, y "las mujeres de vida licenciosa" colocaban una rama en las suyas, de ahí el término "ramera". Todo, aun por el número, es, para el XX, la *ramera*, con un adjetivo sartreano: *respetuosa*: *Detusca et ses gendarmes* entran y cobran su diezmo (y más), su derecho de pernada (y más): para él, todo número y todo nombre es una rama; todo, también la palabra, la insignia dicha ante su puerta, puta, cosa, uso. No participación ni cuidado. Habría que fijar, al menos, una (palabra) que, sabiendo, ignorando lo que es, sea *ni quid ni quod*, nada, o, a lo mejor o peor, singular y nada *respetuosa*, harto irrespetuosa más bien.

Esta *irrespetuosidad* se refiere al arte que se desconoce a sí mismo, o más bien, a los intersticios que hay entre las nociones *déjà vues*, prestigiosas, rentables: no propone incendios ni herejías, no dispone de bomberos ni de inquisidores: descubre el hueso en sí astillado, no hay ortopedia alguna. Ante la tradición: la hembra fecundada por el macho, el onanismo, el terror al incesto,—para decirlo con figuras—, se siente ni pródigo ni bastardo, solamente hijo y dice "sólo se puede dar lo que no se tiene. No hay nada mejor que lo mejor perdido". No se tiene el *plus* del *ya*, ese posible (?) donde en alud confluyen todos los imposibles. Lo perdido, el *antes* y el *después*, se fuga en el instante, es inextricable.

Habiendo mentado a Villon, y a unas figuras de la tradición, se

hovers when imposed, incites when exercised (today consciousness is an object that enters into oscillations of value): it would have increased his *tragic sense of life*. Valéry: *il n'est rien de si beau que ce qui n'existe pas*: that was his venture; for the *Nouveau Petit Larousse*, which to his way of thinking carries it back to reconciliation to the mean, *il commence par publier des poèmes, mais voit dans la litterature une dangereuse idolatrie*: opposing a *but*, accusing of some *danger*. For conjuring both of them they carried him, alive, into the classroom, into academia: Valéry heard an (anthologizable) *mise en scène*, a function of his *Cimetière Marine*: his dysfunction sits far, very far away. Where?

So as not to make this damned enigmatic harangue (?) either too long or too efficient, one invokes two names: Dada, Duchamp: the latter, who delivers the former, bristles on 2 November 1962: "I threw the bottle-rack and the urinal at their heads as provocations, and now it turns out they admire their aesthetic beauty." But *that* admiration, *that* astonishment or wonder, is not a "recognition that one is ignorant" but a mediatization, a "reconciliation between the conservative human being and subversive art" (Moles, Wahl), it's the *kitsch* that "is always in the process of diverting toward rationality" (Hermann Broch). *Beauty, aesthetics* as accessories of function's asceticism and hedonism (made possible through abundance).

I don't know whether Duchamp, when constructing his "green box," was familiar with *Ne lui riblent sa caige vert* (*Le Testament*, CXX, sixth line) by Villon (1431-1463), a title which Carlos Alvar translates as *no le quiten su cajita verde* (*don't take off with his little green box*), noting that for Thuasne, *cage vert* is a metaphor that equates "to a woman of licentious character." Villon asks that *Detusca et ses gen d'armes* not steal her away from him, that they not carry her away from *frère Baude*: beyond the *cage vert*, Detusca and his men have snatched everything from Balde, from Villon, from Duchamp and from you.

In the Middle Ages insignias, rather than numbers, identified the doors of the houses, and "women of licentious character" placed a sprig (*rama*) on theirs, from which is derived the term "ramera." But for the number everything is still a *ramera* for the XX century, with a Sartrean adjective: *respectful*: *Detusca et ses gen d'armes* enter and collect their tithe (and more), their *droit de seigneur* (and more): for this XX century, every number and every name is a sprig; everything, and the word too, the insignia before the door, whore, thing, usage. Not involvement or

cita otro verso suyo: *Je leur ramentois*[2] *le jeu d' âne* (*Le Testament*, CXLVII, octavo verso): *les recordaré el juego del asno*, según Alvar este juego es el del amor. Quedémonos sólo, por esta vez, con la hembra fecundada por el macho, con el asno fecundando a la hembra del caballo: El hijo, el mulo, es estéril—"terror", "obediencia", "secreta paciencia", "desfiladeros": se oye a Lezama en su voz—pero, desde su tara, se fija el mismo autor, *al fin el mulo árboles encaja en todo abismo.*

Pero ¿esos árboles son todos y ninguno, el último y, al fin, el primer árbol: lo *ella*, lo *él* reconociéndose inefables, hoy machihembrados como piezas de una ruptura inacabable y a la vez promisoria, lugar? ¿Ella, él, la obligación, el castigo, las nupcias malditas con lo otro en su eternidad traidora?

¿La vocinglera inadecuación festiva, ritual de muerte, vida, de estas palabras que entre sí no se ven y se desacompañan y mienten y traslucen, qué, no se han servido de otros y otros y otros para regodearse en *su* imposibilidad furtiva? . Sí. No. Al menos se acoge al abandono al que la ha relegado el adelantado, no ser, de nadie, de nada, sólo a la soledad, sólo al abismo, y cita *Le combat avec l'ange* de Jacques Prévert (*Paroles*, 1948):

> *N'y va pas*
> *tout est combiné d'avance*
> *le match est truqué*
> *et quand il apparaîtra sur le ring*
> *environné d'éclairs de magnésium*
> *ils entonneront à tue-tête le Te Deum*
> *et avant même que tu te sois levé de ta chaise*
> *ils te sonneront les cloches à toute volée*
> *ils te jetteront à la figure l'eponge sacrée*
> *et tu n'auras pas le temps de lui voler dans les plumes*
> *ils se jetteront sur toi*
> *et il frappera au-dessous de la ceinture*
> *et tu t'écrouleras*
> *les bras stupidement en croix*
> *dans la sciure*
> *et jamais plus tu ne pourras faire l'amour.*[3]

Imposible *l'amour* con la realidad "arreglada", *le jeu d' âne* que nos quiere recordar, desde su imposibilidad, Villon.

care. One (word) at least should be settled: which, knowing and ignorant of that which is or may be *ni quid ni quod*, nothing, or for good or worse, singular and not at all respectful . . . To rephrase: a word that is maximally *disrespectful*.

This disrespect refers to art that is not self-aware, or rather, is unaware of the interstices between moments of *déjà vu*, the prestigious and profitable moments: it proposes neither arson nor heresies, has no firemen or inquisitors at its disposal: this art discovers nothing but the splintered bone, for which there is no orthopedic cure. In the light of tradition: the fertile joining of female with male, onanism, terror of incest—to say it in symbols—this art understands itself neither as prodigal nor illegitimate issue, just as progeny, and says "you can only give what you do not have. Nothing is better than the lost, best thing." You don't have the supplemental *already*, that potential (?) wherein all impossibilities converge in waves. That which is lost, the *before* and the *after*, escapes in the instant, becomes inextricable.

Having mentioned Villon, and some figures from the canon, I cite another of his lines: *Je leur ramentois*[2] *le jeu d'asne* (*Le Testament*, CXLVII, line eight): *I refer you to the game played by the ass*, according to Alvar the game of love. For now let's just take the female impregnated by the male, here the ass impregnating the mare: The son, the mule, is sterile—"terror," "obedience," "clandestine patience," "the defile": you hear Lezama in his voice—but through its defect the author notices, *in the end the mule slips trees into every abyss.*

Now, are those trees all and none of them, the last tree, and ultimately the first: *she* thing, *he* thing recognizing themselves to be unspeakable, today spliced with tongue and groove like parts of a joint that is at once a break and a promissory, a location? She, he, the obligation, the punishment, the accursed marriage to otherness in its perfidious eternity?

The boisterous and fun-loving inadequacy, ritual of death, life, of these words that don't see each other and leave each other alone and lie and reveal, what, have they not served others and others and others, plentiful in *their* furtive impossibility? Yes. No. At least one embraces the abandonment to which someone forward-looking has relegated the word, not existing, not belonging to anyone, anything, just to solitude, to the abyss, and one quotes *Le combat avec l'ange* by Jacques Prévert (*Paroles*, 1948):

No se coloca una queja, sino una constatación, la servidumbre de un dato. Mentadas al principio las marchas, se va a la más antigua conocida (1040), atribuida a "un Yosef el escriba", finaliza: "Enfermaron ojos alegres / ya duelen con tanto mal". Mil novecientos cincuenta años después de aquellos ojos, que no son necesariamente los de Yosef el escriba, ¿en qué no se habrán convertido? ¿no serán acaso el ojo que ve al XX y, no es necesariamente el de nadie, no lo ve viéndolo?

Para este ojo (si existe y se asiste en sí a sí mismo) todo está inscrito en un quieto devenir. Es vapuleado por lo real real, que termina cuando se pone esta coma, lo real *sido*, que es y ya no es porque se fue al nombrarlo *sido*, y la realidad expectante a ¿qué?, de ¿qué? Sobre este palimpsesto raspa y raspa la uña en *la hora* (que) *es oscura y nosotros como perdidos la vivimos* (Pasolini). ¿*Es*? ¿Qué *hora*? ¿Qué *oscura*? ¿Qué *nosotros*? ¿Qué *perdidos*? ¿Qué *vivimos*?

¿No nos ampara más su disfunción? ¿No nos remite más a su participación y a *su* cuidado? El argumento contrario en su extremo exhibe extremos logros: la bomba de neutrones y a Samuel T. Cohen: la fusión nuclear y su, según él "ocupación fascinante": construir armas: "la mía es una bomba limpia," dice Cohen, hijo pródigo de la *función*.

Toda esta refutibilísima perorata acarrea una sufrida pérdida de la mente, el desaplicado, para el *yo soy* en la Gran Víspera y en el fin (el Pezón, la Nada); tornados deseables, toda víspera, todo fin, también los son sin mayúsculas, aparece el deseo, el afán infinito de unidad imposible, en sí, y en otro, con lo otro; el balbuceo agraz sin don ni parabienes se embulla en este no querer, anhelante a su pesar, y va y vuelve de *aquello*, alma, fe, sentido, sin nombre ni número, de lo cual, todos, somos intermediarios al/hasta el urdir discursos que son lo inteligible dichoso, dicho, hecho, gozo, que acaba en la moneda, en la letra de cambio, la usura, el usufructo que es.

En la raíz de la lengua se recogen unos versos de Ben Al Muallin (siglo XI, segunda mitad): "Alba que tiene tan bello vigor / Cuando viene pide amor". Se va al tercer milenio. ¿Alba? ¿Amor? ¿Podremos darlo? ¿Dárnoslo? No. Sí.

Ángel Escobar
La Habana, 14 de marzo, 1990

Keep out of it
everything is fixed in advance
the match is faked
and when he appears in the ring
surrounded by kleig lights
they'll loudly intone the Te Deum
and even before you're out of your corner
they'll peal the bell for you
they'll throw the sacred sponge
in your face
and you won't have time to fly in his feathers
they'll snow you under
and he'll hit you below the belt
you'll take the count
your arms stupidly stretched in a cross
in the sawdust
and never again will you be able to make love.[3]

L'amour is impossible in a "tidy" reality, *le jeu d' âne* of which Villon wants to remind us with his limitation.

No complaint is lodged. Rather a verification in obedience to fact. Noted at the beginning, the lines move now to the oldest known match (1040), attributed to "one Yosef the scribe," which concludes: "Joyous eyes fell ill / and cause sorrow now with so much evil." One thousand nine hundred fifty years after those eyes, not necessarily those of Yosef the scribe, into what have they not transformed? Are they not the gaze cast upon the XX century, a gaze that may not belong to anyone, that goes unseen while seeing?

For this eye (if it exists and attends to itself) everything is inscribed in an arrested form of becoming. It is beaten down by the real real, which concludes as this comma is placed, that which *has been* real, which is and now is not because it departed with its designation as *has been*, and the reality expecting what? From what? The fingernail scratches and scratches away at this palimpsest in *an hour* (which) *is dark and we live it as if lost* (Pasolini). *Is?* What *hour?* What kind of *dark?* What *us?* What kind of *lost?* What are *we living?*

Doesn't dysfunction offer us greater shelter? Doesn't it submit

1. Uno de los nombres con que se mienta al sujeto posible no se abole ni se oculta, mas bien reseña el gesto de Odisea ante el Cíclope y va al sentido de su traslación simbólica de uno a otro lugar de sí mismo. También se acoge a tres expresiones: no eres nadie; no soy nadie; un don nadie.

2. Rappelle

3. "El combate con el Ángel"—No se vale / todo está preparado de antemano / el match está arreglado / y cuando él aparezca sobre el ring / rodeado de estallidos de luces de magnesio / ellos entonarán a voz en cuello el Te Deum / e incluso antes de que tú te hayas levantado de tu silla / te tocarán las campanas a todo vuelo / te tirarán a la cara la toalla sagrada / y no tendrás tiempo de lanzarte sobre él / se arrojarán sobre ti / y él te golpeará por debajo del cinturón / te desplomarás / los brazos estúpidamente en cruz / en la lona / y nunca más podrás hacer el amor.

to us more involvement and care? The argument coming from the oppo-
site extreme exhibits extreme accomplishments: the neutron bomb and
Samuel T. Cohen: nuclear fusion and *his* "fascinating occupation": the
manufacture of arms: "mine is a clean bomb," says Cohen, prodigal son
of *function*.

Underscoring this enormously refutable harangue is a pro-
longed loss of mind, the equivocal subject, of *I am* on the Great Eve and
at the end (the Nipple, Nothingness); desirable tornadoes, all eves, all
ends, even those without capitalization, desire appears, the infinite thirst
for impossible unity, unity of self, in another, with the other; the nasty
babbling without talent or congratulation roils in this refusal to want,
avid in spite of everything, *it* comes and goes from over there, soul, faith,
sense, nameless and numberless, of which we all are intermediaries
for/until the devising of discourses that are intelligible and auspicious,
said, done, pleasure, all ending in currency, the written exchange value,
usury, and usufruct that is.

Gathered at the base of the tongue are lines by Ben Al Muallin
(XI century, second half): "Dawn with such lovely vigor / asks for devo-
tion when it arrives." The third millennium is coming. Dawn? Devotion?
Will we be capable of giving it? Giving it to each other? No. Yes.

Ángel Escobar
Havana, March 14, 1990

1. [Some footnotes were placed in the original by Escobar.] One of the names with which
one indicates the possible subject; it does not abolish or hide itself, but rather describes the
gesture of Odysseus facing the Cyclops and goes to the meaning of his symbolic shift from
one place to another within himself. It also has recourse to three expressions: you are not
anyone; I am not anyone; a nobody.
2. Rappelle
3. English translation by Lawrence Ferlinghetti. Escobar includes the following translation
to Spanish in his note: "El combate con el Ángel"—No se vale / todo está preparado de
antemano / el match está arreglado / y cuando él aparezca sobre el ring / rodeado de estalli-
dos de luces de magnesio / ellos entonarán a voz en cuello el Te Deum / e incluso antes de
que tú te hayas levantado de tu silla / te tocarán las campanas a todo vuelo / te tirarán a la
cara la toalla sagrada / y no tendrás tiempo de lanzarte sobre él / se arrojarán sobre ti / y él
te golpeará por debajo del cinturón / te desplomarás / los brazos estúpidamente en cruz /
en la lona / y nunca más podrás hacer el amor.

El castigo

Vengan. Les diré: "No es necesario reír".
No es necesario. Yo que conozco el ruido
que prefigura el azar tras los espejos
les diré: "No estoy aquí para alegrarlos".
(Pusieron todos estos muebles. Trajeron
guirnaldas. Y qué bonitas son las luces.
Ah, y estas calles que agradecen los telones.
El fiasco, el ruido, la soledad. Las calles
no eran sólo el resplandor de las fachadas.
Hemos cruzado por sobre esos cuchillos
que a veces dan al mar. Mar y ciudad mienten.
Y mienten esos altavoces solícitos
que alguna vez dijeron: "Si. Seréis Príncipes".
No. Ya hemos pagado el alquiler del número
y del nombre. Y hasta el plagio que comete
la Historia entre altavoces y epifanías
con sus modernas religiones ridículas.
Ay, sólo el amor por ella iba a salvarnos.
Cuántas alcobas habremos adornado.
En la ciudad, en el mar, no en el camino
donde el sol también es un gruñón bastardo
que se pudre. Muebles, guirnaldas y luces
y callecitas pintadas nos invitan
a sacudir las cabezas de los títeres.
Olvidaremos el mar y las ciudades.
Olvidaremos el sol y los caminos.
Olvidaremos sin más los altavoces.
Olvidaremos la soledad y el miedo.
Trajeron todos estos muebles. Pusieron
guirnaldas. Y qué bonitas son las luces.
Hay manos empeñadas en aumentar
nuestra flaca, adusta vocación de olvido.
Colgaron estas campanillas antiguas.
Nos dieron vistosos y aplaudidos trajes.
Aquí salimos. Hay otras manos que —
palmaditas, salud y suerte —, nos dieron

Punishment

Come. I'll tell you all: "You don't have to laugh."
You don't have to. I who know the noise
foretelling the fate behind reflections will
tell you: "I'm not here to make you happy."
(They put out all this furniture. They brought
garlands. And the lights are so pretty.
Ah, and these streets that give thanks for stage curtains.
The fiasco, the noise, the solitude. The streets
were nothing but the splendor of facades.
We've crossed above those girders
that sometimes open to the sea. Sea and city lie.
And those solicitous loudspeakers lie
that said at one time: "Yes. You shall be Princes."
No. We've already paid for the rent on the number
and the name. For the plagiarism committed by
History between loudspeakers and epiphanies
with her ridiculous modern religions.
Oh, only love for her was going to save us.
How many bedrooms will we have decorated.
In the city, on the sea, not on the road
where the sun too is a grumpy rotting
bastard. Furniture, garlands, and colorful
little lights and streets invite us
to throttle the heads off the puppets.
We'll forget the sea and the cities.
We'll forget the sun and the roadways.
We'll just forget the loudspeakers.
We'll forget the solitude and fear.
They brought out all this furniture. Set out
garlands. And the lights are so pretty.
There are hands determined to magnify
our thin, grim vocation of forgetfulness.
They hung these ancient handbells.
They gave us showy suits, much complimented.
Here we appear. There are other hands—
slaps of the palm, good luck and good health — that

días y noches que nos verán cumplir
la ceremonia. Comienza la función.
Sí. Subiremos ahora al entarimado.
Entre los brillos fingidos del atrezzo.
Hoy es bueno tener la cara pintada.
Arriscar la nariz, bizquear. Dar los saltos
de los tontos, de los sapitos suicidas
es inaconsejable. Siluetas pulcras,
caras que todavía resistan el golpe
de los sellos y la sucesión de cifras.
Y sacudir las cabezas de los títeres.
Ya es mucho. Ya es poco. Es nada. Es todo cuanto
de nosotros se espera. Y aquí salimos.
Hoy es bueno tener la cara pintada.
Y hablar mirando los muros, las almenas,
el hierro, el esplendor de las atalayas,
los quepis. Volver luego a las galerías
que paredes azul tierno disimulan,
a la fría celda, al interrogatorio
sutil, la voz bronca del teniente Rosas,
es lo difícil. Por eso es que inventamos
aquí en el patio, aquí, bajo un cielo neutro,
todos los argumentos que os divierten.)
Vengan. Sí. Vengan y les preguntaré:
"Por qué mi nombre se les pudre en la boca".
(He aquí la escena. La luz que golpea el rostro.)
No prometeré lo mejor del pasado.
(He aquí el instante. Las cortinas con pájaros
que por última vez cruzan los encajes.)
No encenderé esas lucecitas que gimen:
Mañana, Mañana, Maña—, nada de eso.
(Aquí en el patio, aquí, bajo un cielo neutro.)
Hoy sé tan sólo la obsesión de un número.
(Que paredes azul tierno disimulan.)
Mi corazón no es el bicho que fascina.
(Supongo que ahora llegan, supongo que
me miran con el derecho que les da
ser otros.) Diré: "Ya este reflector cansa.

gave us days and nights in which to carry out
the ceremony. The function begins.
Yes. We'll step up on the platform now.
Among the feigned sparklings of the props.
Today it's good to have makeup on your face.
To stick your nose in something, to cross your eyes. To
jump around like fools, like suicidal frogs,
is inadvisable. Tidy silhouettes,
faces that still resist the impact
of imprints and the succession of sums.
And to throttle the heads off the puppets.
It's a lot now. It's not much now. It's nothing. It's everything
one hopes to get from us. And here we appear.
Today it's good to have makeup on your face.
And to speak looking at the walls, their decorative tops,
the iron, the splendor of the sentinels,
their kepis. To go back then to the galleries
that warm blue walls conceal,
to the chilly cell, the subtle
interrogation, the gruff voice of Lieutenant Rosas,
that's the hard part. That's why here on the patio,
out here, under a neutral sky, we invent
all the storylines that entertain you.)
Come. Yes. Come one and all, and I will ask:
"Why does my name turn rotten in your mouths."
(Here I have the scene. The light beating against the face.)
I won't promise the best of the past.
(Here I have the instant. The curtains with birds
who cross the lacework for the last time.)
I won't turn on those little lights that whine:
Tomorrow, Tomorrow, Tomorr—none of that.
(Here on the patio, here under a neutral sky.)
Today I know only the obsession with a number.
(That tender blue walls conceal.)
My heart is not some fascinating creature.
(I suppose that now they arrive, suppose
they look at me with the right that comes with
being others.) I'll say: "This spotlight is exhausting already.

Y cansa el diván de Rosas. Cansa el hierro".
Seguirán los soldados en sus garitas.
Ustedes tiesos se lustrarán las máscaras.
Ensayarán sus coartadas de mamíferos.
Y yo, sólo yo, no habré mentido a tiempo.
Mejor me callo. Mejor no digo nada.
O digo lo que aprendimos del libreto.
Me siento junto a un atril, frente al micrófono:
— No olvidaremos llamar a Campanella.
— Nos reconforta tener esta butaca.
(Ni siquiera por ello tendremos menos
motivos para injuriar. Somos el precio.
Esa moneda por la que el camarero
patea a Charlot sacándolo de encuadre.)
Comienzo. (Me temo. Me odio.) Los divierto.
Fúlgidos son los minutos del recreo
y no os libraré de mí ni del olvido.
Vengan. Sí. Vengan y les preguntaré:
"Tengo acaso la biografía de un héroe".

And Rosas' couch is exhausting. The iron is exhausting."
The soldiers will go on inside their sentry boxes.
Rigid, you'll make your masks look great.
You'll display your mammalian alibis.
And I, only I, will not have lied in time.
Best that I shut up. Best that I say nothing.
Or say what we learned from the pamphlet.
I sit down next to a music stand, in front of the microphone:
—We won't forget to call on Campanella.
—We feel better to have this seat.
(Not even for that will we have fewer
reasons to throw insults around. We are the price.
That coin for which the waiter
kicks Chaplain, knocking him out of the frame.)
I begin. (Afraid of myself. I hate myself). I entertain them.
Shining are the moments of leisure,
and I won't free you of me or from oblivion.
Come. Yes. Come and I'll ask you all:
"Do I maybe have the biography of a hero."

La novela de Oersman

Es tarde o no para olvidar — pregunto —.
Y me gritan que sí los álamos. "Hasta luego",
musitan y se van como abuelos distraídos.
Continúa pues la hierba con sus bromas
por debajo del peso de algún muerto,
de algún asesinado.
Es triste o no para olvidar — pregunto —.
Y me miran que sí los perros. Estos
perros. "Llora por unos ojos blancos
que no giran"—bisbisean entre sí, se van bobeando
como perros que son después de todo. Y como todo
este ruido que se pudre en la hierba.
Y como todo torpe acribillado.
Es bueno o no para olvidar — pregunto —.
Y me chillan que sí las rosas y los pájaros,
el mar que no está lejos.
Cuchichean pues los grillos por debajo del peso
de mi cuerpo.
Hay comadres lavando sus rastrojos,
Hay pañuelos de primas percudidas,
Hay un tipo que corre
hasta que un hijoeputa le borra el pavimento,
hay sábanas
y sábanas que pasan sobre nuestras cabezas
y sobre mi pupitre.
Es tarde, triste, es demasiado bueno
para olvidar?
        — No contestaba.
Sólo allá lejos quedan
fotógrafos y guantes bien doblados
junto al quepis.
Y el sonido de botas sobre el mármol.

Oersman's novel

Is it late or not, for forgetting—I ask.
And the aspens call out, yes. "See you later"
they mumble, rambling off like distracted grandfathers.
Well the grass goes on with its waggery
under the ballast of a dead man,
an assassination.
Is it sad or not, this forgetting—I ask.
And the dogs look me a yes. These
dogs. "He weeps through white eyes
that do not revolve"—they whisper in asides; they act
dopey as dogs. Which after all they are. Like all
this clatter rotting in the grass.
Like all who are pockmarked and fumbling.
Is it good, the forgetting, or not—I ask.
And the roses and birds shriek yes to me, and
the sea, not far away.
Then the crickets drone under the ballast
of my body.
There are womenfolk washing stalks,
There are kerchiefs from dirt-stained cousins,
There's a guy who races along until
some sonovabitch erases his sidewalk,
there are sheets and
sheets that sweep over our heads
and across the surface of my desk.
Is it late, sad, is it too good,
for forgetting?
        —No answer.
There, far off, just
photographers and folded gloves
next to the army cap.
And the accent of boots on the marble.

Desde el suelo

Voy a quedarme aquí donde quién sabe.
No puedo ya ser otro—un estudiante acaso
al que fascinan
los hasta luego específicos del viernes—.
Esto es al fin el sol. No hay además,
ni antes,
ni algún día.
Sólo las voces
que poco a poco anulan los emblemas.
Esto que pasa sobre mí son ellos.
Y el azar y su lápiz malogrado.
No es la acuarela con un árbol negro.
Se abre el portillo lejos, suena la casa.
Y el aroma de lilas. ¡Y el pañuelo!
Todo este blancor ciega. Y ciegan
cuchillos que rechinan contra mí.
No hay más allá,
no hay más acá
que esta tosca inversión de los espejos.
Sólo estos jeroglíficos del ruido
que nadie hizo constar en las medallas.
Siguen. Aptos sobre sus botas. Siguen.
Ya cuanto importa sobre mí son ellos.
No es la ventana
desde la que tan mal contábamos
los vagones azules del expreso.
Son ellos. Ellos. Con brío acezante cruzan
por arriba de un simple mueble incómodo.
Nada es, nada es
sino este film oscuro, este pasillo
en que topamos con cachivaches viejos.
La Historia y lo que era, el nombre,
ese jadear remoto tras los libros.
Pasan.
Yo pude haber tenido mejor puestos los pies.

From the floor

I'm going to stay right here where who knows.
I can't be other anymore—a student maybe
fascinated by
the see you later specifics of some Friday—.
This thing is at sun's end. There's no furthermore,
no beforehand,
no someday.
Just voices
that little by little cancel out emblems.
This thing passing over me, it's them.
And chance and its busted pencil.
It's not the watercolor with black tree.
The crack opens far away, the house rumbles.
And the aroma of lilacs. And the kerchief!
All this whiteness blinds. And blinding are
the knives that grind complaints against me.
There's nothing more there,
there's nothing more here
than this basic inversion of mirrors.
Just these hieroglyphs for sound
that no one recorded on coins.
They go on. Able, above their boots. They go on.
Now all that weighs down on me is them.
Not the window
where we'd count blue
express coaches. Badly.
It's them. Them. With shallowbreathed vigor they cross
above this plain uncomfortable furnishing.
Nothing is, nothing is
but this obscure film, this hallway
where we bump against old pieces of junk.
History and what the thing was, the name,
that remote panting after books.
They go by.
I could have been better grounded.

Y el corazón, al menos el corazón.
¡No un almendro en el polvo podrido
y bajo la locura de esta luz!
Marchan. Qué displicente, eterna caravana.
Pasan.
Se abre la mano en el andén penúltimo
clamando como un rostro. Suena la casa.
Siguen.
Acaso no me ven. Ya me tacharon.
Pasan.
Como accidente acabo en el lenguaje.
Oh, nubes,
sólo estos jeroglíficos del ruido.
El ruido.

¡Atrás vienen los tanques!
Lo que existe.
No alcancé a soñar cómo se disuelven
con su esténtor sobrado los afanes.
Ni cómo se disipan los trozos que juntamos
para armar
aquel rompecabezas de la dicha.
¡Los tanques!
El hule
con hipocampos rojos que hay sobre la mesa.
Son las orugas. Vienen. No basta este rumor.
Todo este frío.
Se acercan.
Gris máquina final, torpe diadema,
dile a tu conductor que no es por eso.

Llegan.

Qué mueca así quedar con esta sombra
que me da por la cara cuando salgo
por esta puerta en que se abrilla el límite,
que me da por la espalda en cuanto entro

With my heart, at least my heart in place.
Not an almond tree in corrupted dust
under the lunacy of this light!
They march. Indifferent, eternal traffic.
They go by.
The hand opens on the penultimate platform,
clamoring like a face. The house rumbles.
They go on.
Maybe they don't see me. They already blotted me out.
They go by.
As if accident I end up in language.
Oh, clouds,
just these hieroglyphics for noise.
The noise.

Behind come the tanks!
What exists.
I couldn't have dreamed up the cracking
of desires under stentorian overload.
Or the scattering of the pieces
we had gathered to build
the puzzle of happiness.
The tanks!
The rubber tree
with red seahorses there on the table.
They're the crawlers. They come. This murmur isn't enough.
All this cold.
They get close.
Ultimate gray machinery, awkward diadem,
tell your driver that's not the reason why.

They arrive.

What a look, ending with this shadow
that gives it to me in the face when I go out
by this door, where the borderline was opening,
that gives it to me in the back the moment I come in

por esta puerta en que se anubla el círculo
abierto hasta no ser sino sólo este

golpe!

Oh, rostros que olvidé que me olvidaron.

by this door, where the circle is darkening,
opening until it's no more than this

slam!

Oh, faces I forgot that forgot me.

Apuntes para una biografía de Helene Zarour

Creía en las manos y en la boca, en los eventos
que al espejo remiten al cruzado
antes de que le astillen el cráneo contra el muro.
Creía sólo en el cráneo en el espejo; el muro—
el desconcierto inaugural, el fin, el tizne—
que de un solo chasquido vuelve ininteligibles
los tácitos reflejos bifrontes de obrepticios
cristales, no era más que una extensión del ruido.
Nació en el siglo cuyo orden va del ciego ruido
al ruido. (Ay, quién tolera. Ay, qué te identifica.)
En él murió. (Menos le bastaría a Calímaco.)
Murió es error. Porque aún vuelven las tardes a las tardes.
Y ese sutil defecto de mi voz
difiere los augurios. No se ha ido al mar.
Ahora escuchamos una canción en la que el mar
no es él, sino un olvido sudamericano.
Ahora tiene veinte años. Cree en la Osa Mayor
temblando arriba; en un blue jeans, los sábados y Diego;
en Epictecto comentando a Sartre.
Cree en el té y en los cigarrillos furtivos-
entre ellos vio a Milton—; no sabe que no sabe
de las dobles luciérnagas caribes de las rocas,
ni de la triple exaltación del agua occidental
por un falso crepúsculo. Cree creer que oyó
que hubiera sido reina. (La democracia
a cada quien, mordaz, le otorga un vicio.) Coronada—
así reza el holán fino de la leyenda—,
creía en el eudemonismo de la palabra alfanje.
Sin coronar, en diccionarios españoles olvidó
los simultáneos nombres de Dios, y el páramo
y el día en que una muerte y un Zarour concisan
la inextricable escarcha que a toda la extensión victima.
Al dorso: a la batista la embosca hoy un cuchillo.
A la reina, los cascos de caballos sudados.
El resto se ha perdido en las actas policiales.
Allí no entro: no un sol, el miedo es quien me inclina.

Notes toward a biography of Helene Zarour

She used to believe in her hands and in her mouth, in the events
they transfer to the mirror and crosscut
before they smash her skull against the wall.
She believed only in the skull inside the mirror; the wall—
the inaugural uncertainty, the end, the soot—
that renders the aphonous Janusface reflections
of obreptitious surfaces unintelligible with a single crack.
Glassy, they were no more than an extension of the noise.
She was born in the century whose nature moves from blind noise
to noise. (Oh who can bear it. Oh what identifies you.)
In this century she died. Less would suffice for Callimachus.
Died is an error. Because evenings still return to the evenings.
And that subtle defect in my voicing
differentiates the omens. She has not gone out to sea.
Now we hear a song in which the sea
is not sea, but a Southamerican oblivion.
Now she is twenty. She believes in the Great Bear
twinkling above; in a pair of jeans, Saturdays and Diego;
in Epictetus remarking Sartre.
She believes in tea and furtive cigarettes—
between them she saw Milton—doesn't know that she doesn't know
about the doubled fireflies among Caribbean rocks,
or the triple exaltation of western waters
at an illusory sundown. She believes she believes she heard
she would have been a queen. (Democracy, scathing,
bestows a vice on every one.) Coronated—
she recites the fine frill of legend—
she used to believe in the eudaimonic powers of the word scimitar.
Uncoronated, in Spanish dictionaries she forgot
the simultaneous names of God, and the high plain
and the day on which a death and a Zarour coincide in
impenetrable frost that murders the whole expanse.
At her back: an ambush cuts through the batiste today. A knife.
For this queen, the hooves of sweatsoaked horses.
The rest is lost in the police records.
I don't go there: I'm inclined to follow fear, not sun.

(Mi voz, ni haz ni envés, sólo puede histerizar a Schelling.)
Ahora ya hay un jergón, un sótano con gritos.
Difuminan las mentidas cartografías
del cielo desde el techo las pesadillas y el horror
que el despertar no evita sino más bien provoca.
Chirría un cerrojo ríspido. Sí. Romo
que viene a interrogar. Sí. Pero dónde estarán
las manos y la boca, los eventos
que al resumir el juicio el juicio implora.
Dónde quedó aquel pájaro. Hacia cuáles
rosas sin azar ni causa, innominadas,
reptó el concepto rosa. Nadie puede ya responder.
Nada vuelve a su don. Y hasta la cifra civil—
los guarismos que hoy escoltan la luz, ya sin festines—
yerra su animal público y serpea ociosa.
Rechinó el fiel: al muro, a la razón al uso, al ruido—
no sé: ya se me olvidan los tiempos en que a las tardes
las enlazaba un verbo no una postrimería—,
al exilio francés, al traste, al mar sin joyas—
mal que le pese a Valéry. O a mí que leí *diamant*—.
Cumple, instante, el nada más en que se ahogó mañana.
La oyes: cantará una canción que para colmo
no le correspondía. La ves: a qué mayor castigo.
Al pie; a las manos fláccidas; al pecho el agua.
Y canta. El agua. El agua. Y canta. El borboriteo—
trizas del mundo—, el leve reclamar un afecto.
Hay otra Elena, otro fue, otro allá, y otro comienzo.
Al sesgo nos miramos las ínclitas cabezas.
Con el gendarme salimos de la celda.
Al paso. Todos en uno. Al paso. Al paso. Al paso.
Al paso tu hominidad también. No hay dispensa,
fisgón, tú, puerco deshollinador de doctrinas.

(My voice alone, neither front nor flipside, can unwind Schelling's mind.)
Today there's a straw mattress a cellar with screams.
From the ceiling spurious
cartographies of sky fade the nightmares and horror
that awakening does not dispel, instead provokes.
A sticky bolt would squeal. Yes. Romo
who arrives for interrogations. Yes. But where are
her hands and mouth, the events
that judgment needs when justice resumes.
Where did that bird end up. Toward which
unnamed roses, luckless, without a cause,
did the concept rose crawl. No one can answer now.
Nothing resumes her talent. And even the nonmilitary count—
figures escorting light today, no ceremony—
falls out of its public animal state, snakes along lazily.
It grinds the faithful: against the wall, against acts of reason, against
        noise—
I don't know: I'm already forgetting those times when evenings
were interlaced with language, not by an ending—
against exile in France, utter collapse, against the sea lacking in jewels—
though it irritate Valéry. O and me for I once read *diamond*—.
Mark, instant, the nothingelse in which she drowned tomorrow.
You can hear her: she'll be chanting a song that wasn't even
like her. You see her: for what greater punishment.
To the letter; her flaccid hands; into water up to her chest.
And she chants. The water. The water. She chants. The rumbling—
shreds of world—a faint claim on affection.
There is another Elena, an other was, another out there, another
        beginning.
On a diagonal angle we look at each other, illustrious heads.
With the gendarme we exit the cell.
Walk along. All as one. Walk. Walk. Walk.
Your hominid state walks too. There is no dispensation,
meddler, you, you pig brushing the soot off doctrines.

Gestos

(. . .) la propia compañía. Sobra espacio
y no se ha de perder ningún escándalo
para quien ama escándalo. La música (. . .)
—E. Diego

"No hay playas ni cisternas, no hay otros huecos solos
como diez jubilados cacareando en torno al maíz
de los agromercados"—dice.
Y el hablador del parque deja pudrirse el vaho
de su cigarro entre los dientes—dice—.
Hasta que pase aquella que le pregunte la hora.
Eso además. "Yo no soy un borracho todavía".
—Ya está bueno, ya. Que se callaran coño, dijo—.
Se echa a dormir no en el primer descanso
de la escalera sino en el vano del infierno.
En la playa entre bracitos de muñecas y vidrios masticados
se oye el ruido de las cisternas clausuradas.
Soñamos con mandrágoras y líquenes
con las narices rotas contra el cristal frío.
"De manera que hoy viernes yo me asomo
a todo lo que hierve"—Serguéi Esenin, el tosco Vladimiro,
tú y el otro. Tuvo que ser un viernes de mañana,
y ninguno sabía que alguien ya se había muerto
en el intento. No se habrían suicidado los tres
así como así, o los muchachos que vuelven del colegio
pateando una latica no llegarían sudorosos y sonrientes
a la esquina.

Gestures

(. . .) the company itself. There's more than
enough space and no scandal need be missed
by anyone who loves scandal. The music (. . .)
—E. Diego

"There are no beaches or cisterns, there are no other holes lonely
as ten pensioners crowing around the corn
at the farm market," he says.
And the talker in the park lets the smoke from his cigar
go to hell between his teeth, he says.
Until maybe that woman goes past and asks him the time.
And also. "I'm still not a drunk."
"That's enough, now. Silence goddammit, he said."
He lies down to sleep not on the first landing
in the stairwell but at the mouth of hell.
On the beach between dolly arms and chewed-up glass bits
you hear noise from sealed cisterns.
We dream of mandrake and lichens
noses broken against the cold crystals.
"So that today Friday I look out
at everything seething"—Sergei Esenin, the rude Vladimir,
you and the other. It had to be a Friday morning,
and none of them knew that someone had already died
in the attempt. The three wouldn't have committed suicide
in just any old way, or the boys who come back from school
kicking a can wouldn't arrive at the corner all sweaty
and smiling.

Dos capítulos

I.

Dónde estamos. O para qué quiere mi tranquilidad
toda esa gente. Ay del riesgo, hermanito, el pobre,
el simple riesgo de llevar la cuenta: el número
de muertos sin aviso. "La culpa me matará, y a mi mujer.
Algo nos matará.
No el riñón ni disparos, sino simplemente eso. Aquello
nos matará". Ese día cae una lluvia finísima. Cae
del cielo comprado sobre la tierra rota, cae
como sobre cualesquiera otros lugares comunes
que hacen del hombre el orangután imbécil que fascina.
"Yo estoy borracho por hoy y por mañana, o solo para siempre
y vuelvo a la ciudad." —Y un día se sabe que todo esto
no es más que un argumento—. Algún silbido a veces.
Sube. Va de almendro a blanco consentido. Tonto. Todo.
Sin embargo te esperan. Tu mujer, aquel cloqueo de huesos
en la cama.
No hay que mirarse las manos señaladas
por los griticos rojos del cigarro o el tictaqueo acezante
de tu reloj pulsera. No te vires.
"Dónde estamos. O para qué quiere mi tranquilidad
toda esa gente." El cielo extraño arriba a su manera
y los árboles como blusas tendidas entre el humo y la mugre
de los guardavecinos
no se inclinan por ti. Olvida el viento que te esperan.
"Por eso lanza su entretenida mentira contra los cables
del tendido". Tú y yo sabemos: Nadie. O sólo alguna viola.
Cada noche le debe a otro recuerdo el día que viene.
De nada vale que aquél se vuelva, ansioso, y les pregunte:
Godoy, Pedro, Manuel, a qué se juega. Ay del riesgo, el pobre,
el simple riesgo de llevar la cuenta: el número, hermanito,
el número de muertos sin aviso.

Two chapters

I.

Where are we. Or what do all those people
want with my peace of mind. Oh the risk, little brother, the poor,
the simple risk of keeping count: the number
of the unannounced dead. "The guilt will kill me and my wife.
Something will kill us.
Not a kidney or gunshots, but simply that. The thing out there
will kill us." On that day a very fine rain falls. It falls
from the bought-out sky onto the broken earth, it falls
as rain does over any other common places
that make of man the imbecilic orangutan who captivates.
"I'm drunk today and for tomorrow, or alone for ever
and I go back to the city." And one day you know that all of this
is nothing more than argument.—Some occasional whistle.
It rises. It goes from almond to an accepting white. Stupid. Totality.
However they are waiting for you. Your wife, the clucking of a skeleton
in the bed.
No need to look at your hands highlighted
by the red yelps of the cigarette or the breathless ticktock
of your wristwatch. Don't turn aside.
"Where are we. Or what do all those people
want with my peace of mind." The sky above estranged in its own way
and the trees like blouses hung through the smoke and grime
of ironwork separating balconies
don't bend for you. Forget the wind, they're waiting for you.
"So he throws his amused lie against the wires
of the clothesline." You and I know: Nobody. Or just some viola.
Every night he owes the coming day to another memory.
It's useless for that guy to turn back, anxious, and ask them:
Godoy, Pedro, Manuel: what's the game. Oh the risk, the poor,
the simple risk of keeping count: the number, little brother,
of the unannounced dead.

II.

Manuel, Pedro, Godoy: cuatro, tres, doce velas.
Tú vete a tu mujer, vete a la cama. Vete a la
cuidada gratitud de las proclamas, hasta la vida de hoy.
Vete a la mierda.

Pedro, Godoy, Manuel: cuatro, tres, doce velas.
Tú vete a tu mujer, vete a tu cama. Vete a la
rodilla del cuartel que te reclama, hasta la fiesta de hoy.
Vete a la sala.

1. Mochila
2. Canana
3. Boina
4. Brazalete
5. Collar
6. Blusón verde
7. Pantalón de soldado
8. Saya rosada
9. Saco
10. Fusil
11. Soldado
12. Niño
13. Cinta
14. Peluca: dos

Godoy, Pedro, Manuel: dónde estamos, por Dios, dónde nos llevan.

II.

Manuel, Pedro, Godoy: four, three, twelve candles.
You, go to your woman, go to your bed. Go to the
cautious gratitude of the proclamations, toward Today's Life.
Go to hell.

Pedro, Godoy, Manuel: four, three, twelve candles.
You, go to your woman, go to your bed. Go to the
kneeling of the barracks that demands your presence, toward
    Today's Life.
Go to that room.

1. Backpack
2. Cartridge belt
3. Beret
4. Armband
5. Dogtags
6. Green shirt
7. Soldier's pants
8. Pink skirt
9. Man's suit
10. Rifle
11. Soldier
12. Child
13. Ribbon
14. Wig: two

Godoy, Pedro, Manuel: where are we, my God, where are they taking us.

Tartamudea el ángel

Me abrazas y soy real. Yo no puedo ser otro.
Tú me distingues, y soy eso que se organiza
como un ruido. Sé que estas palabras son
tan feas como inútiles. Yo también soy inútil
y sucedo (sólo porque tú quieres). Antes
miraba Dios o la extensión o nadie, según
yo hubiera sido Berkeley o Spinoza. Ahora
me miras tú. Y yo no soy Karl Marx, ni otro
que lo menciona y me apabulla. No he muerto
en San Lorenzo todavía. En Chatelet no está
mi celda pródiga. No recibí los golpes
que ahora debo. ("Otro minuto es otro ante la usura"—
Y el siglo es fui.) Tal vez me tache esa agresividad
como a un verbo no sé si transitivo. Tú me miras.
Sabes que sé que me dijeron que no tuviera
miedo. Yo, tras la celosía, veo esos cuerpos
sin rostros; te traiciono: ya no sé si me miras.
No sé si soy tu invento o el recelo,
la broma de un sofista. Tú me traicionas.
Veo que pasas junto a esos arduos cuerpos melancólicos.
Yo estoy en esta calle que es la única del mundo
(lo son todas las calles) sin nombre ni argumento
para que en vilo siga clónico la comedia. (Lo mismo
ante ti rezan innumerables versos
que como yo hoy son sagas del olvido.)
Ya no me miras, y cada gesto que urdo va al vacío
de los acápites que rayan las actas policiales.
No sé si voy o vengo, si anhelo soy o asfalto.
Aquí significar no significa.
Nada puedo argüir.
Y aunque viniera, o fuera tu angustia o la calzada—
ninguno de esos gladiolos reconforta. No soy tú,
no soy el sol ni los automovilistas. ("Hay en sí
algo ya nulo", dicen, "la acción en mis metáforas".) Pero
sé que susurran los peatones: "Son las horas esas
ramas". Luego se contonean corriendo al funeral:

The Angel stutters

You embrace me and I am real. I can be no one else.
You make me out, and I'm some thing taking form
like a noise. I know these words are
ugly as they are useless. I too am useless
and happen (only because you want it). Before,
God or extension or no one was watching, according to
whether I were Berkeley or Spinoza. Now
you are watching me. And I'm not Karl Marx, or anyone else
who mentions him and overwhelms me. I still haven't
died in San Lorenzo. My prodigal cell is not
in Chatelet. I did not receive the blows
that I now owe. ("One more minute is one more next to usury"—
And the century is once I was.) Maybe that aggression brands me
a verb, could be transitive, I don't know. You are looking at me.
You know that I know that they told me I shouldn't be
afraid. I, behind the latticework, I see those bodies without
faces; I betray you: now I don't know whether you're looking at me.
Don't know whether I'm your fabrication or a suspicion,
a sophist's joke. You betray me.
I see you go by alongside those grueling, melancholy bodies.
I'm on this street, the only one in the world
(as are all streets) without a name or a storyline
for going along with the comedy, identical and uncertain. (Innumerable
poems pray to you for the same thing;
like me, they're sagas of oblivion today.)
You're not looking at me now, and every gesture I devise goes
into the vacuum of headings scrawled on police registers.
I don't know whether I'm going or coming, aspiration or asphalt.
To signify here does not signify.
Can't point to any evidence.
And if I were coming, or were your angst or the roadside—
none of those gladioli offers comfort. I'm not you,
I'm not the sun or the motorists. ("There's something
already null," they say, "the action in my metaphors.") But
I know the pedestrians whisper: "Those branches are
the hours." Then they run off hips swinging to the funeral:

"Hoy cae el penúltimo acto". Yo (al menos así está escrito)
llevo la cara puesta, la merced de un abrazo. Ellos,
tácitos, me odian (me temían). Es mi talante
el fardo que oblicuo creen gané en una escaramuza.
Cada visaje informa sus actas policiales. Dicen:
"Otro minuto es débito"—y me ofrecen sus máscaras.
El sueño aquel de Dafnis o algo los estremece.
Quizá sea el ojo que no logran sacar los cuervos
de mis fotografías. Quizá tú no caminas
entre esos arduos cuerpos melancólicos.
Quizá es otro el que repite en los visillos
la ilusión de tu nombre y de tu abrazo. Quizá
tampoco existes y yo no me organizo. Otro no
nos ha soñado absorto en sus persianas, ciego al brillo.
Y no, no hay esta imprecación incómoda. No hay tercero.
No hay música.

"The penultimate act falls on this day." I (or so it is written)
adopt a face, bring the mercy of a caress. They,
unspoken, despise me (were afraid of me). It's my disposition,
oblique, a bundle they think I won in a skirmish.
Each grimace informs their police proceedings. They say:
"One more minute is the debit"—and they offer me their masks.
That dream of Daphnis, or something, makes them shudder.
Perhaps the eye the vultures can't get out
of my photographs. Perhaps you're not walking
around among those grueling melancholy bodies.
Perhaps it's another man between lace curtains who repeats
the illusion of your name and embrace. Perhaps
you don't exist either and I am not taking form. Someone else hasn't
dreamed us up, absorbed in his shades, blind to brightness.
And no, this irritating curse isn't there. No third is there.
There's no music.

Siempre escasea un relámpago en la mesa

Llueve. Al fin y al cabo hasta el cielo empalaga.
Y aquí se vive como al centro de un día
con los bordes comidos por los pájaros.
Alguien ríe. Alguienes se desnudan en un cuarto de hotel,
junto al mar cascarriento que ha venido
con más huesos de ahogado este domingo.
Ella se lava los pies echados a perder. O está en la casa
sola, sola,
sola y desnuda también como un pistoletazo.
Mirándose los pies.
En cambio tú y yo no nos conocemos todavía.
Y aquí se duerme como en el último banco de una estación
cualquiera,
desde la que han salido el primer tren y el último
hace un rato. "Si usted mira por los visillos
de la ventana afuera
verá los raíles torcidos como moño de viuda".
Después no pasa nada. Llueve.
Y la cuñada del esposo de la otra
se limpia pues las uñas bostezando. "Llueve"—
dice quien no está lejos—. Con todo y eso
aún no nos reconocemos. Es otro quien allá telefonea—
"Te digo que no puedo contarte el argumento"—.
El aire entra a escurrirse en los zaguanes,
choca contra los bultos que hay agazapados
y nos palpa la cara como un ciego. Ya nos vamos.

Always a shortage of lightning on the plateau

Rain falls. When it's all over even the sky seems sticky.
And here you live as at the center of a day
with edges nibbled off by the birds.
Someone laughs. Others undress in a hotel room
by the squalid sea that rolled in
this Sunday with more bones from the drowned.
She washes decomposing feet. Or is in the house
alone, alone,
alone and naked as a gunshot too.
Looking down at her feet.
By contrast you and I don't know each other yet.
And here you sleep as if on the last bench of any old
station,
from which the very first train and the last both left
a while ago. "If you look through the curtains
of the window out there
you'll see rails twisted up like a widow's chignon."
Afterwards nothing happens. Rain falls.
And the sister-in-law of the husband of the other woman
cleans her nails, yawns. "Rainfall"—
says someone not far off. In spite of all this
we still don't recognize ourselves. It's someone else there on the phone—
"I'm telling you I can't explain the scenario."
The air enters and slides through the hallways,
bangs against the forms crouched there
and gropes at our faces like a blind man. Now here we go.

Veintiuno y diez. Me fijo

Los muertos están muertos.
Muertos y agujereados como simples colmenas.
Ni siquiera las manos les transpiran.
Son otros, son—quiero decir—los vivos los que hablamos.
Los que mentamos un nombre en las aceras,
y nos hacemos cómplices del agua
que pasa entre sus huesos humillada.
Pero los muertos, los muertos están muertos.
Tranquilos, y bien aclimatados al silencio que no los desespera.
Los muertos se olvidaron de sus ganas.
Y los otros—quiero decir—seguimos, meramente de novios,
de compinches, de jefes o almas buenas.
Nos cambiamos de acera y vestimenta.
Nos tocamos las manos o los hombros, nos besamos los ojos
y seguimos, seguimos murmurando de nuevo en otra acera,
meneando como loros borrachos las cabezas cansadas,
tropezando volteados cual hormigas contentas de sus días.
Mientras los muertos siguen en su tumulto a solas.
Atorados de oficios y percances, bien o mal o a deshora
se encontraron con el silencio aquel que los ha mordido.
Los otros escuchamos renuentes las campanas: dón-de es-tán?
Ya se sabe cómo abriremos luego el fósforo
para el antepenúltimo cigarro de la última congoja.
Y volvemos ay—quiero decir—volvemos de nuevo a las aceras
a engordar los saludos, las prisas y los ruegos.

A poco se nos gasta el rumor.
El impulso se nos hace de pronto
el puñadito de sal que quiere la vecina.
Y el murmullo incesante de las horas se vuelve,
se vuelve—quiero decir—se ha vuelto
esa sorda colilla que un pisotón apaga.

Twentyone and ten. I see

The dead are dead.
Dead and full of holes as your basic beehive.
Not even their hands perspire.
They are others, they—I mean—the living, we who speak.
We who mention a name on the sidewalk
and turn accomplice to the water
that moves, demeaned, among their bones.
But the dead, the dead are dead.
Tranquil, and well acclimated to silence that causes them no despair.
The dead forgot their desires.
And the others—I mean—we go on, merely as fiancés,
or as buddies, bosses, good souls.
We change our sidewalk and clothing.
We touch hands or shoulders, kiss each others' eyes,
and go on, go on muttering again on some other sidewalk,
waggling tired heads like drunken parrots,
stumbling topsy-turvy as ants carefree all their days.
While the dead go on in their tumult alone.
Choked with offices and mishaps, for good or bad or at the wrong time
they met up with distant silence that bit them off.
We others listen unwillingly to the bells: now-where are-they?
You know already how we pull out a match
for the second-to-last cigar of the final sorrow.
And we go back oh—I mean—we go back out again to the sidewalks
to fatten up our salutations, our rushing around, our pleading.

Soon the rumor runs down.
The momentum suddenly turns
us to a pinch of salt that the neighbor wants.
And the incessant muttering of the hours comes back,
comes back—I mean—it's back in
a deaf cigar butt that a stamp blacks out.

El escogido

Sobre esta piedra está mi cabeza.
Y sobre mi cabeza está la luna.
Saber eso no reconforta a nadie.
Menos aún saber que sobre la luna
hay otra cabeza y otra piedra.
Y que la suma de actos y palabras
que he cometido terminaran aquí.
En otra cabeza, otra piedra y otra luna
que no son ni estas ni aquellas
que por desidia y vanidad mentábamos.
Esto no me separa de mi destino:
El día, la noche, el animal y el límite.
Hay además qué corva infinitud donde
la cabeza es la piedra y la piedra
es la luna. Lunas, cabezas, piedras
no son conjuntos sucesivos. Ni son
las caras de mi cara en el lago.
Sé que sólo los ruidos en que ardo se suceden.
Y que sólo mi discurso es dado al espectáculo.
Sé que cada una de estas proposiciones
vuelve inútiles las cabezas, las piedras
y las lunas de los mayores. Y sé
que la conclusión de alguno inutilizará
las mías. Hoy todo arquetipo es vano.
No necesito ya ninguna justificación
entre los símbolos. Voy a morir.
Mi cuerpo es sólo un cuerpo acuclillado.
Nada saben ni la blanca explanada
ni el cuchillo. Sólo por mí repiten
su intercambiable suma de razones.
No eran el filo y la extensión, sino sólo
lo que aquí me esperaba. Ni los pasos ni el tacto,
ese rescoldo, el gusto de caminar y ver
y tocar y bien decir me hacen invulnerable.
No evitan las antorchas ni esta última hora.

The chosen one

Above this stone is my head.
And above my head is the moon.
That knowledge makes no one feel better.
Much less the knowledge that above the moon
are another head and another stone.
And that the sum of acts and words
I've performed may end here.
In another head, another stone and another moon,
which are neither close nor far
which we used to mention with apathy and pride.
This does not divide me from my destiny:
The day, the night, the animal and the line.
Moreover, what curve infinitude exists where
the head is the stone and the stone
is the moon. Moons, heads, stones
are not consecutive sets. Nor are
the facets of my face in the lake.
I know: only the crackles in which I burn follow.
I know: only my discourse is given for the spectacle.
And: each one of these propositions
renders the heads, stones
and moons of the elders useless. And I know
someone else's conclusion will render mine
useless. Today all archetypes are empty.
I no longer need justification
among symbols. I am going to die.
My body is just a body squatting.
The white esplanade and the blade
know nothing. Their interchangeable
combination of reasons pulsates through me.
They were not the sharp edge or extension, merely
something awaiting me here. None make me invulnerable,
not the steps or the contact, not those hot coals,
the pleasures of walking and seeing and touching and speaking well.
They can't fend off the torches or this final hour.

Sólo yo sé mi nombre, sólo yo sé
de la obsesión de un número.—Buscan y hallan
nombre y número el centro en donde no hay más
que otros nombres y números y eclipses—.
Me matan. Lo hacen como si yo fuera otro.
Mi sangre topará con los terrones
filosos que jugando juré que eran
la prefiguración de los cuchillos.
Ahora son los cuchillos. No hay juego
ni juramento que no hayan sido el juego
y el juramento que ahora signan mi muerte.
A toda esta ceremonia la llaman
sacrificio. Ah, yo también hurgaba
entre los peces de los días, las cifras
y las nomenclaturas. Yo también vi
imágenes demasiado veloces para el sueño.
Intuí una orden que no era la vigilia.
Fui lo ínfimo. Fui la totalidad.
O creí intuir y ver y ser. Ahora
mi cuerpo es sólo un cuerpo en el que chocan
luz y sombra y se acabó y no vuelvas.
Pero entre candelas y ojos miro y ardo.
Soy lo que fui. Soy lo que no seré.
Soy realidades excesivamente arduas:
Lunas, cabezas, piedras, ceremonias.
No quiero saber que huyen, no quiero saber cómo
las cosas a hurtadillas se escapan de sus nombres.
Voy a mentir, voy a mentir como se miente:
"Están ahí. Y ahí me son ajenas".
No. El ajeno soy yo. Tampoco alegra
imaginar que acaso mi muerte estaba escrita
y que alguien, en su lugar, parsimonio, lee:
"El fugaz dardo ya se olvidó del arco.
Desconoce si hay un capricho más:
Desliz, esplendor, máscara u objeto".
Es mi muerte. Mi muerte. Esa es mi muerte.
Todo se acaba. Oh, no. Ay, pirámide. Ay, luna.

Only I know my name, only I know
obsession with a number. They seek and locate
name and number the center containing no more than
other names and numbers and eclipses—.
They slay me. As if I were some other.
My blood will run off among the jagged
lumps, peaks I swore in jest were
presages of the blades.
Now they are the blades. There's no jest
or oath that has not also been the jest
and oath signifying my death.
To all this ceremony they give the name
sacrifice. Ah, I too picked through
the fish of days, the sums
and nomenclature. I saw
images too quick for dream.
I intuited an order that wasn't vigilance.
I was the lowest. I was the totality.
Or so I believed I intuited saw and existed. Now
my body is just a body where light and shadow
clash and it's over and don't come back.
But among candles and eyes I look on and burn.
I am what I then was. I am what I will not be.
I exist as excessively arduous realities:
Moons, heads, stones, ceremonies.
I don't want to know they escape, don't want to know how
things went sneaking off from their names.
I will tell lies, lie as one lies to oneself:
"They're right here. Here, alien to me."
No. The alien is me. Nor does it give joy
to imagine that my death was written,
that someone in his own space, unhurried, reads:
"The fleet arrow has already forgotten the bow.
It doesn't know if there's one last inconsistency:
Slip, splendor, mask or object."
It is my death. My death. That is my death.
All comes to an end. Oh, no. Ah, pyramid. Ah, moon.

Continúa la espiral. Continúa el círculo.
Y qué, si en espiral y círculo me apago.
Vienen. Lo harán. Yo, lo escogido. Ya ni excepción
ni norma. Me aferran. Todo lo que temí
me envuelve. Todo lo que anhelé me acoge.
Insolencia, pavor, anhelo, error acuden.
Son este blanco y terco día entre
todos los días. Son el minucioso tajo
del cuchillo. Son esta franja oscura y son
este recinto donde lo más arduo es
no poder escapar del conocimiento.

The spiral goes on. The circle goes on.
And so what if, spiraling and circling, I burn out.
They arrive. They'll make it. I, the chosen thing. No longer an exception
or a norm. They anchor me. Everything I feared
shrouds me. Everything I desired takes me in.
Insolence, dread, yearning, error arrive,
present as this white and obstinate day
among all the days. They are the blade's meticulous
slit. They are this dark border and this
enclosure where the most arduous thing of all is
the inability to get away from knowing.

La visita

Es verdad que a los veintiséis años no soy más
que un vecino
asomado a su balcón prestado entre balcones.
Quién me mira desde allá abajo y quién lo mira a él
desde aquí arriba.
Pudiera ser que sea yo este dualismo recalcitrante y tonto
que nos ronda.
Que esté en el pasto allá triscando bejuquillo
y aquí mordiendo otro cigarro amargo.
Esto es acaso hacer práctica muda
de vejez defraudada así como defraudadora.
Esto es acaso el miedo o la cabrona mentira
de los años.
Vivir y ver cómo huyen
en puntitas de pie aquellos esplendores.
Saber que ahora son sólo patrimonio local de los sobrinos.
Quién me dice lo que es toda esta bulla.
Este no más poder seguir siendo el de al lado.
El tipo con ojeras que aplasta su cigarro en el cantero.
El comediante, el sordo o el dormido
en la glorieta de algún parque municipal y público,
vencido. Y no. Sólo salvado de la última visita. Y no.
Porque ahí viene, ya vienen—
después de esos pasitos que raspan con desgano la escalera
seguro que nos sacudirá un aldabonazo—.
                              Ahí suena.

The visit

True, that at twenty-six I'm nothing more
than a neighbor
leaning on his borrowed balcony among balconies.
One who looks up at me from down below, and who looks down at him
from up here.
Could be that I'm this recalcitrant and stupid dualism
encircling us.
That I'm there on that field gamboling among vines
and here chewing at another sour cigar.
This is perhaps making a policy of silence
on aging both defrauded and defrauding.
This is maybe the fear or the perverse lie
of the years.
Living and seeing how those splendors
run off on tippytoes.
Knowing that now they're just local patrimony for the nephews.
Who can tell me what all the noise is about.
This not being able to go on as the guy next door.
As baggy eyes who crushes his cigar into the flowerpot.
The comedian, the deaf guy or the one sleeping
under the arbor at some public city park,
defeated. And not. Just saved from the final visit. And not.
Because here it comes, here they come—
after the quiet steps scrape the stairwell with their indifference
a warning rap will surely jerk us up—.
                                There's the knock.

La edad

Alicia, ya Lewis Carroll te dejó. Y ahora,
ahora eres tú quien corre, la que indaga
debajo de una piedra. Hay manchas
y límites torcidos. Hay otra imagen y otra,
y hay otro espejo y rostros y muñecas
recitando una historia de borrachos.
Hay gorriones—una vez vi un candil—y hay
ómnibus apáticos.

Domingo. Dominó. Domine. Deus.

Blanca, Blanca Armenteros,
Alicia te dejó.
"Toma tu píldora"—húyete
me dicen.
—Di el paso al frente y ahora
ya está
dado
　　al frente al frente al frente
　　al lado al lado al lado
　　al frente al frente al frente
　　al lado al lado al lado

Blanca, Blanca Armenteros.
Ya Lewis Carroll qué sé yo.

The era

Alice, Lewis Carroll took off on you. And now,
now you're running around looking
under stones. There are stains
and torqued borders. One image follows another,
and another mirror and faces and dolls
reciting some tale about winos.
There are sparrows—once I saw an oil lamp—and there are
apathetic omnibuses.

Domingo. Dominoes. Domine. Deus.

Blanca, Blanca Armenteros,
Alice took off too.
"Take your pill"—and get out
they tell me.
—I took a step forward and now
it has been
tried
    forward forward forward
    to the side to the side to the side
    forward forward forward
    to the side to the side to the side

Blanca, Blanca Armenteros.
Lewis Carroll ah. Who knows.

Hospitales

Yo vi a Rimbaud amarrado en una cama
y al Papá Protagónico amarrándolo duro,
y su piyama, soltándolo—gritaban y se soltaron
los huesitos vírgenes con doctores soplando
el fagot roto,
se quebraron los vasos, las persianas, los símbolos
y luego a cada cual según su síntoma
le entregaron su píldora, sus ojos, su cuaresma.
Era el año bisiesto de estos días de marzo y vi
como se ahorcaba el chivo en un pedrusco.
El choncholí explotando su cercado, y él sentado
mirando por arriba—
responsabilidad y culpa a los teléfonos,
a los viejos modales de los jueces
y a sus hijos. Yo vi a Rimbaud escupiendo
en una cesta de ojos bien templados,
y sanos como agujas. Lo vi. "No me
arrepiento". Estoy tranquilo, soy
el escriba, el buey
que no ha tenido nada. Estoy tranquilo.

Hospitals

I saw Rimbaud roped to a bed
and the Paterprotagonist roping him down hard,
and his pajamas, letting him go, they roared and
his smallest innocent bones came loose with doctors
blowing on that broken bassoon,
the glasses shattered, and the blinds, and the symbols
then to each according to his symptom
they gave his dose, his eyes, his Lenten discipline.
It was March in leap year and I saw
the goat choking on a piece of rock.
Big black bird, scapegoat exploiting his enclosure, and he sat there
looking upwards—
the responsibility and blame to the telephones,
to the old ways of the judges
and their children. I saw Rimbaud spitting
into a basket of eyes well tempered
and wholesome as needles. I saw him. "I do not
repent." I am composed, I am
the scribe, the ox
who has not owned a thing. I am composed.

Graffitti

Tuve una casa, una ciudad, una provincia, un país.
O la vanidad que perdió a Gilles de Rais me hizo afirmar
que eran míos. En sucesivos atlas, tan precarios
como minuciosos, me señalé con ellos.
Fui una cruz o una raya, o un círculo cuya imperfección
testimoniaba la traición de mis nervios
y el error de los atlas. La práctica deficiente
de esta pictografía asustada y el juicio
exagerado sobre mí no me hicieron comprender
sino ya tarde que era yo quien les pertenecía.
Padecí una puerta, un parque, un río, y un idioma
que era todas las puertas, todos los parques y un río.
Esa certidumbre, el vértigo, el abuso del lunes
me cegaron. Creí palpar en mi lomo las inscripciones
que antes con displicencia urdía en los mapas.
Me esforcé. Pero la cruz, la raya, el círculo
que sobre mí ejercieron su mandato
demostraron ser un inescrutable jeroglífico
cuya prolijidad delataba el desdén de su ejecutoria
y la suma de equívocos que toda inversión de órdenes
comporta. Sin querer escapé de esas figuras.
Hoy no las hago en parte alguna. No las haré.
Creerme marcador o marcado
en la brumosa rosa de los eventos
que el pagado de sí llama la vida
fue otro pequeño gran malentendido. Creí:
Los documentos, sellos y delimitadores que requisan
la aventura recíproca de los sitios
y del sitiado animal con recuerdos que soy
se tornarán irreales. Giré en torno al alto
de sus pliegos. Impugnables, todo cuanto el azar
o la necesidad habían cometido entre nosotros
era una tercera caligrafía, otro sobrado código
donde lo irreal fui yo y fueron mis nostalgias
de lugares. Acaté ese argumento. O me sometí a él

Graffitti

I had a house, a city, a province, a country.
Or the same vanity that doomed Gilles de Rais led me to affirm
that they were mine. In consecutive atlases, uncertain
as they were meticulous, I took these for signs of my self.
I was a cross or a stripe, or a circle whose imperfection
testified to betrayal by my nerves
and to the errors of atlases. The defective practice
of this terrified pictography and its overdetermination
of my existence did not yield the insight until
late in the game that it was I who belonged to them.
I suffered from a portal, a park, a river, and a language
that were as all portals, all parks and a river.
The certainty, the vertigo, abuse of a Monday
blinded me. On my back I thought I felt inscriptions
I had previously contrived on maps, indifferent.
I worked hard at it. But the cross, the stripe, the circle
exercising their command over me
unfolded in an inscrutable rebus
whose prolix neatness disclosed the scorn of their noble sentence
and the sum of errors that all investment in orders
involves. Without wanting to escape those figures I did.
Today I don't draw them anywhere. And won't.
To believe myself the marker or the marked
in the blurry rose of events
that the cocksure labels as a life
was another wee whopper of a misunderstanding. I believed:
The documents, stamps, and demarcation that
requisition the reciprocal affair between locations
and the animal me located in self-remembrance:
these will turn unreal. I revolved around the high
command of their sealed documents. Unassailable, all
that fate or necessity had trumped up among us
was a third calligraphy, another unnecessary code
in which the unreal part was me, my nostalgia
for locations. I obeyed that plotline. Or it mastered me

por haber olvidado los tópicos
de mi educación dogmática. O por no encontrar otro
que justificara las cenizas de mis ocupaciones
y de mis días. Ignoro si en verdad pude vivir
veintiocho años o soy tan sólo el fruto
de la prodigalidad y el sentido común
de mis contemporáneos. Se daban a entusiasmos tales
y a tan disímiles creencias que puede que yo
y esta discordia hayamos sido una de esas creencias,
uno de esos entusiasmos. Quizá necesitaron
mi fantasma para soñar el acuerdo
entre lo arduo de su producción de ininteligibles
sofismas y la improbabilidad de su hermenéutica.
Pero alguien o algo toma esta cuchilla de rasurar.
Alguien o algo termina en Sitiocampo u Oklahoma,
bajo la luna de Siberia, en Piura o Praga. Sólo esto
que me aniquila aquí—entre el aserrín y las bombillas
fluorescentes, entre las piedras de olor y los espejos—
continúa. Y su repetición te involucra. También
a ti, oh inmundo. En los hoteles de acceso limitado
o en tugurios mugrientos. Al menos
eso necesito creer. Ahora. Cuando antes de morir
escribo todas estas sandeces en la pulcra pared
de un baño público.

para María Elena Diardes

for having forgotten the clichés
of my dogmatic education. Or for not finding another one
to justify the ashes of my occupations
and my days. I don't know whether I really lived
twentyeight years or am just the fruit
of the prodigality and common sense
of my contemporaries. They were given to certain enthusiasms
and such dissimilar beliefs that I and this discord
may have been one of those beliefs,
one of those enthusiasms. Maybe they needed
my phantom to imagine an accord
between the difficulty they produced with unintelligible
sophisms and the improbability of their hermeneutics.
But some one or some thing takes up this razor.
Someone or something ends up in Sitiocampo or Oklahoma,
under the moon of Siberia, in Piura or in Prague. Only this,
annihilating me here—among sawdust and fluorescent
bulbs, mirrors and scented stones—
repeats. And its repetition involves you. You, oh
unclean too. In the restricted-access hotels
or in grimy hovels. Or so I at least
need to believe. Now. When before I die
I scribble these stupidities on the tidy stall
of a public toilet.

for María Elena Diardes

Huéspedes

No me riñen; vienen a tocarme la boca.
Ya habrá tiempo para desbaratarla de un pisotón
o una trompada. Ahora palpan mi boca.
La escudriñan más acuciosos que odontólogos.
Se van. Vuelven, se topan los hombros y como al desgaire
chocan contra ella con la impunidad de los murciélagos.
Todavía eso es tocar. Tocar, tocar la boca.
(Mi madre la lavaba con apazote.
Pero ha salido. Su último, desportillado plato
quedó a merced de esta roña asaz fregado.
Mañana la veré cuando mis huesos—
que no son los de François Villon
ni los de Benjamín Moloise y nada
prefiguran—pendan de su mañana y de su hueso.
Cuando la boca que hoy no abro entre en mi boca.)
Vienen, fatuos, a mí. Letras serán de cuál basto
protocolo. De uno en uno, de a dos, en tumulto
llegan. Sonríen al visorio de la puerta.
¿Les abro? Entran con sus arreos en casa—
donde comparto el número de serie con los muebles—;
fingen una fatiga, algún anhelo, gripes
que les otorgan una coartada invulnerable.
Se sientan o deambulan sigilosos sin ser sombras.
(No hay fantasía ni fábula. Donde se dice:
entrar, entran. Ya para Byron vivificar
discretamente pechos era un infierno.)
Les brindo té, café, cigarros que ya saben
que son suyos como el riñón o los zapatos.
Lustran sus relojes casi cumpliendo un vaticinio.
Chillan opiniones que cobrarán luego a mi angustia:
"Viva en el poeta de veras", me dice uno,
"aquella actitud rebelde a cualquier método".
Yo soy mudo. Giran sus ojos. Tiemblo. Me muestra
unas tijeras. Me mira como a un animal muerto
y se alza. Coge, riendo como en un film silente,

Guests

They don't scold me; they come to touch my mouth.
Later there will be time to deface it with a stomp
or blow. Now they palpate my mouth.
They scrutinize it more diligently than odontologists.
They leave. They return, bump shoulders and, as if careless,
bang against it with the impunity of bats.
A bang: still a kind of touch. Touching, touching my mouth.
(My mother used to wash it out with apazote.
But she went away. Her last chipped plate
was left at the mercy of this overscrubbed piece of filth.
Tomorrow I'll see her when my bones—
which are not the bones of François Villon
nor those of Benjamin Moloise, and foretell
nothing—hang from her morning and her bone.
When the mouth I don't open today may get inside my mouth.)
They come, fatuous, to me. Scripts from whatever rude
protocol. One by one, by twos, in a tumult
they arrive. Smiling in the scope of the door.
Should I let them in? They enter bringing harnesses into my house—
where I share a serial number with the furniture—
they feign fatigue, some form of longing, fevers
giving them an unbreakable alibi.
They sit down or walk about, stealthy but not shadows.
(There's no fantasy or fable. Where one says:
enter, they enter. For Byron discreetly
vivifying breasts was already hell.)
I offer them tea, coffee, cigars they know to be
as much theirs as my kidney or my shoes.
They polish their watches, almost fulfilling a prognosis.
Squeal out opinions for which they'll charge in anguish:
"In the true poet," one says to me, "may the attitude
of rebellion survive by any means."
I am mute. Their eyes roll. I shudder. He shows me
a pair of scissors. Looks at me as if I were a dead animal
and rises. Smiling, like in a silent film, he grasps

un puñado de tierra de una maceta próxima.
Me lo lanza a la cara. No ha ido al jardín ni al campo.
"Uno demasiado cuidado", se dispensa.
"El otro excesivamente áspero". Taconea,
y con sarcasmo me restriega las manos en la boca.
(Sé de gestos que la racionalidad atribuye a Praga.
Sé del vidrio y el polvo; y sé que no sé cuándo
uno u otro son extensión en lo cósmico o reflejo,
ni cuál copia del otro la aberración y el límite.)
Cuál escalofriante dibujo esconden sus medallas
sin objeto. Cuál gestión abusada de mandatos
cumplen contra el *error* de creerse indivisible.
"Tildaron su actitud al hablar de principesca.
Es absurdo que lo expulsaran del periódico".
(A quién dirá que yo dije decir que me dijeron.)
"La libertad es Orgón que por Tartufo inquiere".
(Por qué untar en mi boca el roto azufre
de rastrojos frenéticos—jadear podrido, furia
en fuga, insectos que remedan sus lejanas
categorías en desuso—.) Por qué me escogen.
No soy, ni puedo ser, poeta. No he recibido aún
el certificado. Tiene razón quien tacha
mi nombre en los diplomas. Junté palabras
que ni la vanidad ni el juicio de hoy toleran.
(Mañana, ayer no invoco. Un roce anula el tiempo.)
Me incomodan las líneas que firmé como si fuera
otro. Ni para Rimbaud hay otro. El mito
es ciego. Fragmentos soy, y ruidos. A pesar mío
nunca he violado el blanco, a qué aullar a mi boca
entonces, perros tan orgullosos de sus métodos.
(No soy Hamlet para ajustarlos a la bruñida
plata de Shakespeare—luego caigan de bruces
malogrando el brocado de una sutil cortina—.)
He ensayado la forma de sentarme o reírme,
de mirar. No tengo acceso a los periódicos.
No sé ya si *libertad* alguna categoría es
o un genocidio. Pero vienen a buscar mi boca.

a fistful of dirt from a nearby flowerpot.
He throws it in my face. Hasn't gone to the garden or the countryside.
"One is too careful," he diagnoses.
"The other, far too surly." He stamps a heel
and sarcastically rubs his hands against my mouth.
(I know about gestures that rationality attributes to Praga.
I know the glass and the dust; and know I don't know when
one or the other is cosmic extension or reflection,
or which copy of the other is aberration and limit.)
Their pointless medals hide a horrifying picture. What
an abused operation of command
they wage against the *error* of believing themselves indivisible.
"They branded his attitude, when speaking, princely.
Absurd they should expel him from the newspaper."
(To whom will he tell that I told my telling they told me.)
"Freedom is Orgon inquiring after Tartuffe."
(Why smear the broken brimstone of frenzied stubble
onto my mouth—corrupt panting, fury
in flight, insects that mimic their distant
unused categories—.) Why do they pick me.
I'm not, can't be, a poet. I still don't have
the certificate. Whoever crosses my name off
diplomas is correct. I collected words
of which neither vanity nor today's judgment tolerates.
(I don't invoke tomorrow, yesterday. A little rubbing cancels time out.)
The lines I signed as someone else make me
uncomfortable. Not even for Rimbaud is there an other. Myth
is blind. Fragments am I, and noise. To my regret
I've never hit the mark, why yowl at my mouth
then, dogs so proud of their methods.
(I'm not Hamlet, to fit the methods to Shakespeare's
burnished silver—where they'll fall flat,
spoiling the brocade of a subtly draped song—.)
I've rehearsed ways to sit down here or burst out laughing,
ways to take a look. Don't have access to newspapers.
Don't know whether *freedom* is a status
or a genocide. But they come looking for my mouth.

Ejecutan su ballet perentorio. Valen premios.
Ante mí escurren su diligencia inapelable.
Cuál otra culpa o deuda o pena ignoraré
y, entre retratos y máximas, exorcizarán
el prestamista y el ladrón a pescozones.

Execute their peremptory ballet. Are most worthy of prizes.
Before me they wring out their diligence deaf to appeals.
I'll remain ignorant of any guilt or debt or pain
and, between portraits and maxims, they'll exorcise
moneylender and thief with their wallops.

Así en la paz

"Se me acabaron los peros que traía entre manos,
pero aquello parece que son gentes"—dice el orate
y vuelve la cabeza
y yo empiezo a dudar de mis cabales.
Aquel que viera su mueca de dolor
donde a más de doler le faltan tuercas
y sepa cómo aprieta la cuchara en el plato
y la vira hacia el fondo de la sopa
y él se tuerce en el bulto de la cara
y se vira también con la cuchara
peleando con el plato entre la sopa,
empezará a dudar de sus cabales.
"Vieras cesar entonces el relajo entre gordos.
Gatos bajo el alero. Entré en la bolsa y vi
cómo eran ellos"—dice el orate
y vuelve la cabeza.
Aquel que me oye y yo nos sacudimos negro
el polvo. Nos miramos tocándonos los ojos.
Nos besamos y
saltamos de una vez a un descampado.
Allá lejos, pitando, se pierden los cabales
entre el humo y el sol que ahora enceguece
y da contra las piedras
y rebotando se nos mete en las manos
diciéndonos que sí, que sí, que no queda remedio,
que hay que hacerlo.

In peace

"The howevers I had in hand ran out,
but over there it looks like people"—says the lunatic
swiveling his head
and I begin to doubt that I'm in my right mind.
Whoever might have seen his grimace of pain
where beyond just hurting he's missing some screws
and knows how he presses his spoon against the plate
and turns it toward the bottom of the bowl
and twists the blurry form of his face
and swerves with the spoon
fighting with the plate through the soup,
will begin to doubt that he's in his right mind.
"So you saw the end of the scrap between big men.
Cats under the eaves. I got into the sack and saw
how they were"—the lunatic says
swiveling his head.
Me and the guy who hears me beat out the black of
the dust. We look at each other touching eyes.
We kiss and
leap in one bound to the clearing.
There far away, hissing, the right minds disappear
between the smoke and the blinding sun, now
the sun strikes the stones
rebounds to our hands
telling us yes, yes, there's no alternative,
we've got to do it.

Beulah

El humo y las nubes sobre la ciudad.
Y sobre mí mi nombre.
Las torres suspendidas, los edificios altos,
los postes desperdigados
como suspiros de huérfanos
sobre la tierra.
Y sobre mí tu nombre,
tus dos brazos, los pechos, la boca sacudida
por palabras sangrientas.
Las colillas, los fósforos quemados,
los cartones de ayer,
los confettis, las serpentinas que enamoran los pies
sobre el asfalto.
Y sobre mí la gestión de los cielos amarillos—
tu recuerdo.
Los dientes picados, los horrendos zapatos,
el perro que llega, los tipos que ladran
en malogradas mesas consentidas
sobre losas lavadas, vueltas a lavar
y luego
percudidas por los escupitajos sordos de ahora.
Y sobre mí tú sola.
O con tu fiesta viajando en auto-stop
hacia provincias cercanas o lejanas.
Tú cerca, tú lejana como una maldición
que me persigue apenas con dos manos—
tus ojos.
Tus dos ojos. Sobre toda la tierra.
Y sobre mí, los míos.
Y sobre mí, yo mismo. Aquel, aquel, aquel
a quien ya nada perdona.

Beulah

The smoke and the clouds above the city.
And above me my name.
The suspension towers, tall buildings,
poles scattered
like sighs of orphans
over the land.
And above me your name,
your two arms, breasts, mouth pounded
by bloody words.
The stubs, burnt matches,
yesterday's boxes,
confetti, streamers wooing the feet
on the asphalt.
And above me the measure of the yellow skies—
your memory.
The decayed teeth, the awful shoes,
the dog approaching, types who bark
at pampered tables strewn all
across washed-down stones washed down
all over again and
dirtied by muffled hocking, now.
And above me you alone.
Or with your party, hitchhiking
toward nearby or distant provinces.
You nearby, you distant as a curse
that follows me using only two hands—
your eyes.
Your two eyes. Over all the land.
And over me, my eyes.
And over me, I myself. That guy, that one, that one
whom nothing forgives now.

Los cuatro cuentos

"Tú y yo nos vamos a morir temprano.
Tú y yo nos vamos a morir mañana.
No mañana, hoy. Quizás ya estemos muertos".
Me dijo con cansado paso y gestos
que remedaban lo que dirá el verso
último de mi sueño. Al descampado
dos sombras (ya no son inusitadas
puesto que tú las ves y las vio el claro
ojo de esta patraña que no acaba),
dos sombras—al envés del argumento:
a diario salen miles de los Metros—
éramos. Él me hablaba como un preso
le habla a otro preso sin hablar: retazos
que mi prolijo olvido, esa otra araña,
borró cumpliéndose a sí mismo un pacto.
Sólo a ese olvido la memoria alcanza.
(Te dejo a ti, lector, en zona franca.
Y al que nunca verá, su franja blanca:
... ...)
Fatiga ser dos sombras. Menos cierto
no es el agobio que le dan al cuerpo
del que ambulando se harta de reflejos
en una ciega habitación, y en vano
grita, sonriendo a su inconstante Habana,
como un rey de ajedrez: "Ya no estoy muerto".

The four stories

"You and I are going to die young.
You and I are going to die tomorrow.
Not tomorrow, today. Maybe we're already dead."
He told me with a tired step and movements
that evoked what the final stanza
of my dream will tell. On open ground
two shadows (no longer rare
since you see them, and so does the clear
eye of this tall never-ending tale),
two shadows—on the underside of the storyline:
every day thousands of them exit subways—
two were we. He talked to me as one prisoner
talks to another prisoner without talking: snippets
that my longwinded oblivion, that other spider,
wiped out, fulfilling a pact with itself.
Memory arrives only at obliteration.
(I leave you, reader, in a duty-free place.
And to the one who will never see, I leave his white space:
... ...)
Exhausting to be two shadows. The pressure
they exert is no less evident on the body of the man
out there walking around, who sickens of reflections
in a blind room, and calls out
in vain, smiling at his fickle Havana
like the king in a game of chess: "I'm not dead anymore."

But on, but on, mira la jaula

"El viejo se pasea, y sus legañas
son menos evidentes que sus asertos
de un día", dice. Y el viejo se pasea
por entre los muros blancos de su casa.
Son bonitos los días. Ah, son bonitos
los otros muchos años. Hoy le trajeron
sol. (¡El roce de la luz sobre la mano!)
¿Volverá aquel atardecer casi lila—dice—
cuando entraba? No. Todo este rencor mata.
"Tose. Se muere", alguien lo mira riendo.
Sin embargo él pasea. Quizás el aire afuera
haga muecas baratas entre los álamos
mugrientos, aplastados por el plomo insidioso
del relente. Sin embargo él pasea. "Y es obvio
que los estorninos restriegan y restriegan
sus colas contra los azulejos". (Yo no sé
qué hago aquí. Nadie supo jamás del viejo
ni de mí. Ni de estos torvos pájaros
que entre piar y piar
a diario aplastan las cabezas de jóvenes traidores.)
Aunque uno vaya bajo el humo y la candelita
de su fósforo húmedo los ve. Panza
arriba. Es brutal. Comedimiento. Hay otro.
Los pasillos retocan su agónico
qué tal en las baldosas. Los estorninos
giran. Y el roñoso persiste en mover
su monumento. Dándose palmaditas
como pizcas de sal en las caderas
dice entre sí: "También yo soy los otros". Y los otros:
—*But on, But on, déjalo, quítalo, déjalo.*
—*But on, But on, quítalo, déjalo, déjalo.*
—*But on, But on, quítalo, quítalo, quítalo.*
Ven. Ven, homicida, y raspa el mármol ciego. Ven.
Dame el frío de las vísperas, la soga y la percha
sin destino. (No sé qué hacíamos allí.

But on, but on, look at the cage

"The old man takes a walk, and the sleep crusting
his eyes is less obvious than his daily
insights," he says. And the old man walks around
within the white walls of his house.
Beautiful, the days. Ah, beautiful
the many other years. Today they brought him
sun. (The way the light grazes his hand!)
Will that faraway sunset return, almost lilac—he asks—
as it entered? No. All this hostility kills.
Someone watching him jokes, "He's coughing. He's dying."
But still he walks around. The air moving outside
may pull mean faces among the grimy
poplars, weighed down with the insidious drag
of nightly dew. But still he walks around. "And obviously
the starlings scrape and scrape
their tails against the tilework." (I don't know
what I'm doing here. No one ever found out about
the old man or me. Or about these glowering birds
who crush the heads of young traitors,
chirp to chirp, each day.)
Even if someone slips between smoke and the tiny flame
from a wet match, he sees them. Belly
up. It's savage. Civility. There's another one.
The halls replay his agonized
how are you across stone tiles. The starlings
circle. And the skinflint persists in moving
his monument. Giving himself pats
like pinches of salt on his hips
he says to his selves: "I am also the others." And the others say:
—*But on, But on, leave it be, let him be, leave it be.*
—*But on, But on, let him be, leave it be, let him be.*
—*But on, But on, leave it be, leave it be, leave it be.*
Come. Come, killer of men, and scratch at the unseeing marble.
    Come along.
Give me the cold of evenings, the rope, the perch

Saberlo en cambio es, pues, otro percance
que huele a funeral. Lo más complejo.
Algo así como que se te caigan los ojos,
no se rompan, y alguien los vea rodando
con esa sinuosa opacidad que tiene un tope de hombre
en contradicción
con las muy bien lustradas losas del recinto.) Queman. Y:
"*Hireling day*", dice, "intruso. Topa. Topa. Intruso".
Nadie supo jamás por dónde entraron.

with no future. (I don't know what we were doing there.
On the other hand knowing it is, well, another mishap
that reeks of funerals. The most complex.
As if your eyeballs fell out,
and didn't break, and someone saw them roll around
with the devious opacity of a man's pate
contradicting
the burnished flagstones of the premises.) They're burning. And:
"*Hireling day*," he says, "intruder. Banging. Banging. Intruder."
No one ever found out how they got inside.

Otro texto sobre otra prueba y otra prueba

Manuscrito helicoidal. Así lo llama Rene Francisco. Argumenta tener razones para ello. No las dice. Él lo encontró. Él me lo ha regalado. Razones que intuyo, si no suficientes, excesivas. Cuatro cosas me extrañaron en el texto: el autor se hace pasar por mí (?); procura reconstruir el monólogo de una conciencia en otra (antes lo intentó mejor Borges—aquí leído—y, antes de Borges, Browning, Dante, Platón, un hombre en Altamira); la voz detrás de la voz del hablante no ve, sabe que no alcanza su objeto, en cambio cree posible que éste, José Lezama Lima, sí vea su precaria grafomanía y lo desdeñe; hay, por último, cierta compulsiva admiración por Lezama que no oculta reticencia ante lo crucial barroco (aprendida tal vez en otros). Probablemente me equivoque, y sean otros hitos los que excusen mi oficiosidad. (Aún así, inútilmente, yo la duplicaría.) La del autor aparece dedicada a un tal Eduardo Ponjuán de la Coloma, *tout trouvé.* Es la que vale. Transcribo:

JOSÉ LEZAMA LIMA

Nada puedo argüir. Ya soy igual al igual
que intenté. Sé que no me justifican
esa Habana que construí en La Habana,
ni el ruido en que deambulo ni la urdidumbre ciega
que soy. Sé que otro intentó mi soledad inútil:
Góngora. Y otro miró por mí en mis ojos a otro:
Mallarmé acaso, un griego o no francés.
Yo fui el que fui. Hay una noche que ignoro,
un día que me excluye. Una tarde y dos puertas
vuelven menos precaria mi modestia.
Ya no vuelvo a fingir sabiduría.
Me fascinó el vacío, y aquella espera, y nadie—
insisto que alguien tiene que llegar.
No tuve miedo. Detrás de una cláusula sola
cometí una biblioteca. Ahora fatiga
la prolijidad de la Isla en la Isla.
Dije que no.

Another text about another proof and another proof

Helicoidal manuscript. That's what René Francisco calls it. He argues that there are reasons for it. Doesn't give them. He found it. He gave it to me. Reasons that I intuit, albeit insufficient ones, excessive ones. Four things surprised me in the text: the author passes himself off as me (?); he tries to reconstruct a monologue by one consciousness within another (tried before and better by Borges—read here—and before Borges, Browning, Dante, Plato, a man in Altamira); the voice behind the voice of the speaker does not see, knows it doesn't achieve its object, instead thinks it possible that this José Lezama Lima in fact sees his precarious graphomania and scorns it; there is, all told, a certain compulsive admiration for Lezama which doesn't obscure some reticence (perhaps learned from others) toward the decisive baroque factor. I am probably mistaken, and instead other landmarks excuse my unofficial inquiry. (Even so, pointlessly, I would duplicate it.) The author's appears with a dedication to one Eduardo Ponjuán from La Coloma, *tout trouvé.* This is the one that matters. I transcribe:

JOSÉ LEZAMA LIMA

I can't point to any evidence. I already equal the equal
I intended. I know they don't justify
that Havana I raised within Havana,
or the noise in which I wander or the blindly threaded warp
that is me. I know someone else attempted my futile solitude:
Góngora. And another looked through me with my eyes at someone else:
Mallarmé perhaps, a Frenchman Greek or not.
I was the one I was. There's a night I haven't known,
a day that excludes me. An afternoon and two doors
render my modesty less precarious.
Now I don't turn back toward pretending wisdom.
The nothingness fascinated me, and that hope, and no one—
I insist on someone's pressing arrival.
I wasn't scared. Behind a single cadenced clause
I perpetrated a library. Now the longwindedness

Quién creerá rondar en la metamorfosis,
lo que digo y no digo. Nadie. Nada. Ausculto.
Evaporar el gallo, ni a mi doble crepúsculo
consigo.
Sólo es inmune el tiempo, y el cero de los mayas.
De pronto una mañana tuve y desperté y fui
Calímaco. A la noche lloré mentado en casa
por Beatriz. El olvido me está vedado.
El sol ahora es el sol, no un embullo ni un símbolo.
No puedo escapar del conocimiento.
Soy mi sola memoria, sin sorpresa.
El buscado esplendor: ni la extensión ni el Otro:
El Otro era yo que me esperaba. Vuelvo a escribir:
Dánae teje el tiempo dorado por el Nilo.
Ya no seré aquellos que seré sin darme cuenta.
Vuelvo al retintín del diálogo entre Platón y Arturo.
Vuelvo a la pregunta, a la misma pared, al *tokonoma.*
Los pasillos son los pasillos, el sueño es sueño,
el cazador es cazador. Shakespeare es Shakespeare;
antenas dictan y hay bombillas encendidas
en lo que llamé *bosque congelado*;
el tobogán desciende y la herrumbre
es la herrumbre del cuchillo del réprobo.
No hallaré ya otra relación. La misma utopía
vuelve. Vuelve el *pro domo sua.* La aridez
vuelve. Y este Ángel Escobar, de intolerables versos,
hace que vuelve a lo imposible del idioma
mi nombre que, como lento colmillo al muslo,
no me deja.

of the Island within the Island is tiresome.
I said no.
Who will believe they're circling the metamorphosis,
what I say and do not say. No one. Nothing. I auscultate.
Not erasing the rooster, not getting my doubled
sundown either.
Only time is immune, and the Mayan zero.
Then one morning I had and woke up and was
Callimachus. When night fell I cried, celebrated at home
by Beatrice. Oblivion is taboo for me.
Now the sun is the sun, not revelry or symbol.
I can't escape the knowledge.
I am my lone memory, with no surprise.
The intended splendor: not the extension or the Other:
The other was the me awaiting me. I go back to writing:
Danaë weaves golden time along the Nile.
Now I won't be all the ones I'll be without figuring it out.
I turn back to the dialogue jangling between Plato and Arthur.
I turn back to the question, to the same wall, to the *tokonoma*.
The hallways are the hallways, the dream a dream,
the hunter a hunter. Shakespeare is Shakespeare;
antennae pronounce and lightbulbs are there, lit up,
in what I named a *frozen forest*;
the sledge descends and the rust
is the rust on the reprobate's knife.
I will not find another form of relation. The same utopia
returns. The *pro domo sua* returns. The aridity
returns. And this Ángel Escobar of intolerable poems
causes my name to return to the incapacity of language;
like a slow tusk sinking into my thigh
it doesn't pull out.

Funny papers

Dionisos, Nietzsche, tú y el Crucificado
son el mismo. Y yo quiero alcanzarme
por perderme. No en Dionisos, Nietzsche,
ni en ti ni el Crucificado. Irás a estar desnudo
en la vidriera y, ciertamente, *because the world
is round*, todos te dan su dinero—el cielo azul
y la tierra podrida, y yo, el blasfemo
hediondo, con una pistola descargada
y una bolsita de heliotropo—flores, madera
o jaspe. Tendrás los pies hinchados, Ciego.
Tú mismo eres el Oráculo—no mientas. Pones mis pies
sobre la hierba helada; pero yo estoy en verano,
en el Este, cuando me ve Lucian Blaga. (Oh, Sanguis,
se nos carían los dientes, los ojos se nos ponen
rojos; vamos sobre una moto; nos magullamos
contra un árbol) ¡Edén! ¡Edén! ¿Qué es
lo que me aniquila? ¿Qué es? (¿Qué es lo que falta
ahora?) Tú tienes los pies rotos, tres chelines,
un botón pendenciero y
siete palmos de tierra; entonces los demás se embullan.
Hay un disparo que te busca y corre. ¡Corre! ¡Corre!
Ven a mí. Te he dicho que vengas (y no llegas).
Tienen las manos sucias y un cuchillo mohoso.
Dicen: "Dijeron que seríamos inmortales". *Gun—*
y bailan. *Gun, gun, gun.* Baila, baila,
Réquiem, baila.
Él cae. O el fuego. "Nosotros estábamos desayunando."
Sujétalo. Sujétame. Sujétalo—dicen.
Yo no sé. (No hay el frío de la víspera y, el destino,
aúlla el pobre perro contra el otro arriba.)
Digo que (o dices o dijeron):
Yo no sé cómo pude haberte visto,
Oh Andress Pierglass, dulce bastardo,
sobre ti mismo hacienda esa maroma. —En cambio,
un día escribí que una mujer cumplió

Funny papers

Dionysus, Nietzsche, you and the Crucified
are one and the same. And I want a path to my self
through self-loss. Not in Dionysus, Nietzsche,
not in you or the Crucified. You'll go on to nudity
set in stained glass and clearly, *because the world
is round*, everyone gives their money to you—the sky is blue
and the earth decayed, and I, stinking with
blasphemy, hold a discharged pistol
and a pouch of heliotrope—flowers, wood
or jasper. Your feet will distend, Blindman.
You're the Oracle—don't lie. You set my feet
on frozen grass; but when Lucian Blaga spots me
it's summertime in the East. (Oh, Sanguis,
our teeth were rotting out, our eyes are turning
red; we ride around on a motorcycle; we get battered
against a tree) Eden! Eden! What is
this element annihilating me? What is it? (What is
missing now?) You have broken feet, three shillings,
a button for trouble and
seven handwidths of ground; then the others set the party off.
A shot seeks you out and lets fly. Fly! Fly!
Come to me. I've told you come (you don't make it).
They have dirty hands and a rusty old knife.
They say: "They said we would be immortal." *daDum*—
and they dance. *Dum, dum, dum.* Dance, dance,
Requiem, dance.
He falls. Or the fire does. "We were eating breakfast."
Hold him down. Hold me down. Hold him down—they say.
I don't know. (Last night's chill is gone, and fate,
one wretched dog wails at another above.)
I say (or you say or they said):
I don't know how I could see you,
Andress Pierglass, oh sweet bastard,
working that miracle over yourself. By contrast
one day I wrote: a woman reached

veinticuatro años. Eso, y que Abril no es el mes
más cruel ni yo *il miglior fabbro*—. Olvídalo. Olvídalo.
Blake y Beulah te esperan; también un hemistiquio
en el sur numerado, y la segunda línea de un estrofa
japonesa—olvidaste las tres restantes, Sesqui,
y la sevicia siberiana. A ti. A ti. (Nadie me oye.)
Incordio, Chucho—sólo oyen los que espían las conversaciones—
Lana, ¿también tú puedes morirte tan campante?
¿Y qué me queda a mí? *Because you are round,*
you are round, ¿qué es lo que me transtorna a mí?
No soy un hombre y medio, Cherif. Tengo miedo.
Me vienen a buscar como si yo fuera otro. Se ríen
y me llaman "profesor" porque es que juego mal
con esa caja, es cierto. Acaso—
"Tú eres un negro sucio que no agradece tanto",
me dicen. *Dóctor.* Y se oye:
patamuchta parce que nein nihil nonún.
Por la mañana oímos el periódico, leemos la radio. No.
No. Por la mañana no; a toda hora—eso nos reconforta.
El verdadero héroe de nuestro tiempo
es la televisión. Y somos oportunos y arribistas. Sí.
No. Te digo que no. No hay otro. Pobre San Agustín—
Ahora es un policía. (Míralo allí. Te mira.) A mí, a mí
me mira. Como yo soy un imbécil digo:
Pascal cruza la esquina por donde hay una valla.
Es en tu barrio. Y agrego:
Pero la justa pobreza de nuestra casa,
que es el alibi, el indio, doble nueve,
no se puede jugar agachado,
multiplica el terror de las esferas. Y las esferas—
¿No podrías volverme absolutamente loco, Juan?

age twenty-four. Wrote too: April isn't the cruelest
month, I'm not *il miglior fabbro.* —Nevermind. Nevermind.
Blake and Beulah are waiting for you; plus a hemistich
in the numbered south, and line two of a Japanese
strophe—you forgot the three remaining, Sesqui,
and the Siberian violence. To you. To you. (No one hears me.)
Nuisance, Chucho—the only ones who hear are spying on
    conversations—
Lana, can you expire so composedly too?
And what do I have left of me? *Because you are round,*
you are round, what disturbs me so?
I'm not a man and a half, Cherif. I'm scared.
They come around as if I were someone else. They laugh
and call me "professor" because I play badly
with that box. It's true. Hardly—
"You are a dirty negro who is not so very pleasing,"
they tell me. *Doctor.* And one hears:
patamuchta parce que nein nihil nonún.
In the morning we listen to the newspaper, read the radio. No.
No. Not in the morning; at all hours—it gives relief.
The real hero of our time
is the television. And we're opportunists and arrivistes. Yes.
No, I tell you no. There is no other. Sad Saint Augustine—
now he's police. (See him there. Looking at you.) At me, he's looking
at me. Being an imbecile I say:
Pascal crosses a corner where there's a railing.
In your neighborhood. And I add:
But you can't play the just poverty of our house,
which is the alibi, Indian, a double-nine,
by hiding your best dominoes;
it multiplies the terror of the spheres. And the spheres—
Juan, can you not make me truly insane?

Abuso de confianza

No me has visto. Siglo. Siglo. Oh, prestidigitador.
Al lado de la carpa inmensa venden
barquillos. ¡Y algodones de azúcar!
Y dicen: "Ya estamos hartos de tus opiniones".
No me has visto. No has venido a preguntar por mí,
el de los dedos cortados. Yo era dos muchachos
corriendo. Los remos junto al agua blanca,
el jadeo, sudorosos, y el no hallar suficiente aquello
de las estatuas sepultadas. Qué querías—
era correr sobre las manos negras, los pies rotos
hasta el filo del agua, hasta el filo del agua.

Oh, reino frío. No sean joyas los hierbajos podridos
que refracto. No sean dadas aún mis confesiones.
Por ellas, sólo por ellas, tú has condecorado
a aquél de más. Y yo preferí ser el húmedo campante
que huye. El trapecio y las gradas, y las victorias,
y tus actas policiales: ¡Vaya plácemes! Es evidente:
Yo he podido morir, no deshacer el exceso de la razón
y el uso. No al tropezar con la piedra el muslo, el mito,
las caras de los gladiadores. Dicen: "Eso sería suficiente".
O aquello de que a uno le bastan un transistor
y una ventana, un transistor y una ventana.

Éramos las espaldas cuando empezamos eso. ¡Basta!
¡Basta! La música y el camino resecos—el fardo
al que le dice no a los parabienes y la clemencia
al listo—, pero tú no ves cómo levanto el arco. Lejos
de los comedores donde hay líderes juntando las cabezas
para el final feliz del espectáculo. El plexo solar
sobra; no tu yesquero, mi cigarrillo, las sonrisas.
Diles, Príncipe: Huraños, lenguaraces bastardos. Y a mí:
Mentira que de un solo mal no escapas. Los otros
en el calor se aburren, por ejemplo. Salen de camiseta,
balanceando los brazos. Salen. Balanceando los brazos.

Breach of trust

You haven't seen me. Century. Century. O, prestidigitator.
Next to the big top tent they sell
ice cream cones. And cotton candy!
And they say: "We've had enough of your opinions."
You haven't seen me. You haven't come to ask after me,
after stubbyfingers. I was two boys
running. Their oars close to the whitewater,
panting, sweaty, and not finding that thing about
the buried statues sufficient. What you wanted—
was to run over the black hands, the broken feet
to the water's edge, to the water's edge.

O, cold kingdom. May they not be gems, these rotten weeds
I am refracting. May my confessions not be given yet.
For them, just for them, you've celebrated
that other one all the more. And I chose to be the chill humidity
that gets away. The trapeze and grandstands, and the victories,
and your police registers: well congratulations! It's clear:
I've managed to die, not to unmake the excess of reason
and use. Not when I bang my thigh, the myth, the faces
of the gladiators against the rock. They say: "That would suffice."
Or that line about how it's enough for one to have a radio
and a window, a radio and a window.

We were the backing when we started that. Enough!
Enough! The music and the way dried up—the package
negated congratulations or clemency for the clever—
but you don't see how I'm founding the ark. Far
from the diningrooms where there are leaders putting their heads together
for the spectacular's happy ending. The solar plexus
is unnecessary; not your lighter, my cigarette, the smiles.
Tell them, Prince: Misfits, insolent bastards. And to me:
A lie, that you can't escape a single sin. The others
in this heat get bored, for example. They go out in undershirts,
arms swinging. Go out. Arms swinging.

Miran hacia lo alto. Un edificio. Y otro. Y otro.
—Eh, tú. A nosotros nos gustan los relojes automáticos.
En realidad (¡Simón! ¡Simón!) no me aprendí las reglas—
sólo alcancé la paz que se otorga a los huesos
del conejo, el borboteo del oso
que alguien insiste ahogar en la bañera—. Podrían cesar
el brillo ahora, y los ademanes con excesivo vetiver de las doncellas.
Y así como separan los codos los camareros y van, y van y vienen
en esa retahíla, nosotros nos percatamos: Escupimos
sobre su litografía. No fue el padre de aquellos quien ordenó
desfallecer. Así no. Nadie más vuelva a fila. Nadie más.

Yo me allego al horror del que estoy hecho.
(¿Van los pobres ramajes que me golpearon
loco en la carrera a prescindir de mí?)
Veo tu pulmón rosado. Veo el hielo y la gangrena
de tus vísceras. Sé de los aptos para lustrar
las mascarillas de oro. Sé del trasiego que me expulsan;
"Él ve, él ve la repetición incesante de muertes no marciales".
—¡Hey! ¡*Il sole non si muove*! —Ja. Bailando. Sudan como chicos.
Hacen las alharacas de los picaneados por ti.
Mienten: "Oh! ¿qué es esto? ¿Un hombre tapado?"
Giran: "¿Ves algún dios detrás de mí?" ¿Ves algún dios?

Chillan. Arriscando los labios. *Il sole non si muove*.
Salta. Y dice: "Maldita cosa qué me importa".
Enola Gay tenía un pubis tan tierno (el Organon)
como Albertine en Spoon River. Y: "Ya hemos
explicado por qué ello es así". ¿Habrían
de importar los excesivos tics nerviosos, Franz?
Vivimos adornando con potes de cerveza la Analogía
de Kuei Mei. Tal vez eso nos reconforta. Al haragán
empleado de banco, al traidor. *Le pendu*, el fusilado—
de Beulah comentábamos con ganas de astillar
las vitrinas—: Qué pocas las pepitas. Gritan: "Fuego! ¡Fuego!"

Y ya. No hay casa para nosotros. Ni siquiera la otra

They look upwards. One building. And another. And another.
—Oh, you. We like the self-winding watches.
In reality (Simon! Simon!) I didn't learn the rules—
I only got as far as the peace granted to the bones
of the bunny, the bubbling of the bear
that someone insists on drowning in the bathtub—. The glittering
could end now, and the excessively perfumed expressions from the maidens.
And just as the waiters lift their elbows and go, and go and come
in that stream, we perceive ourselves: We spit
on his lithography. It wasn't the father of those guys who ordered
the loss of heart. Not like that. No one else gets back in line. No one.

I gather myself to the horror out of which I'm made.
(Will the miserable branches that beat me
crazy during the race dispense with me?)
I see your rosy lung. I see the ice and the gangrene
in your entrails. I know about the abilities to show off
the golden masks. I know from the shuffling that they're throwing me out;
"He sees, he sees the incessant repetition of non-military deaths."
—Hey! ¡Il sole non si muove!—Ha. Dancing. They sweat like boys.
They do the song and dance of the people tortured by you.
They lie: "Oh! what's this? A man concealed?"
They spin: "Do you see some god behind me?" Do you see some god?

They squeal. Their lips up to something. *Il sole non si mouve.*
Jumps. And says: "Damn thing what do I care."
Enola Gay had a pubis as tender (the Organon)
as Albertine in Spoon River. And: "We've already
explained why that is." Did the excessive
nervous tics have to matter, Franz?
We live adorning the Kuei Mei Analogy
with jugs of beer. Maybe that brings us comfort. To the idle
bank employee, to the traitor. *Le pendu,* one shot by firing squad—
we talked about Beulah with the desire to smash
shop windows—: How few nuggets there are. They shout: "Fire! Fire!"

That's it. There's no house for us. Not even the other one

a un paso de los farallones, la de los platos azules
del borracho. Sólo el desfiladero es para mí. Y las piedras
que prefiguran el agua. ¿No lloré acaso por todas
esas sonrisas que me cercaron?: "Sin embargo
eres tú quien pone el nombre". ¿Yo? ¿O Juan Inaudi?
¿Un edificio? ¿Y otro? ¿Y otro? No. Se sigue siendo
el orangután imbécil que fascina.
¿Acaso somos aquellos camareros para llevar—
ay los gladiolos. Ay, el pelo de las muchachas
púberes—y traer las vísceras así? ¿Así no más? ¿Así?

"Dos muchachos corriendo". Es evidente. Y alguien
los ve pasar, sudoroso. Ahora bien: Nosotros somos
el tercero. Incluso digo que nadie nos espera; ni a Dios,
ni a la Naturaleza: Excelentes paraguas rotos—
en medio del trasiego de insecticidas—.
¿No lo querían? Me he detenido a sopesar
las utopías histéricas, dividendos y usuras.
(Es la puerta cancel. Veo al cruzado.)
Las caras sobre los pergaminos. (No eran.) Y ya.
(Los dedos que entran.) Dicen: "El barro tan filoso
hiere". Y en verdad hiere. El barro tan filoso hiere.
Estas palabras no son para ti. Yo no juego
en la arena. No estoy en un aeropuerto internacional
pateando una caja vacía de *Original Russian Vodka*.
Ni me rajé la cara con una botella rota. Yo no cargo
a mi hermano. Ni a ningún otro muerto. Yo no me cargo
a mí. Las olas muerden. No hay ni un puñadito de candor.
Tu ojo me ve bailando sobre el filo de las imprecaciones.
La arena es la que es verde, el mar arena. Duermen
tres; cuatro te hablan; dos mil se hacen añicos. Sólo uno,
entre el cristal del trópico y la esperma del lunes, vocifera—
y eso que está de vacaciones, que está de vacaciones.

No soy yo. No eres tú. No son cuatro ni tres.
Ni dos mil. Ni los posibles datos del Obispo,
nuestra computadora. También tú buscas enemigos,

a step from the crags, the house with the drunkard's
blue plates. Only the ravine for me. And the rocks
that foreshadow the water. Didn't I cry for all
those smiles that enclosed me?: "However
you are the one who does the naming." Me? Or John Inaudible?
One building? And another? And another? No. Still
the imbecilic orangutan who fascinates.
Maybe we're those waiters to carry—
o, the gladioli. O, the hair of pubescent
girls—and to bring entrails like that? Just like that? Like that?

"Two boys running." It's clear. And someone,
sweaty, sees them go past. Well now: We are
the third person. I even say that no one is waiting for us; not for God,
not for Nature: Excellent broken umbrellas—
under the downpour of insecticide—.
They didn't want it? I've paused to consider
the hysterical utopias, dividends and interest fees.
(It's the inner door. I see the crusader.)
The faces above the scrolls. (They weren't.) That's all.
(The fingers that enter.) They say: "Clay that hungry
hurts." And it truly hurts. Clay that hungry hurts.
These words are not for you. I'm not playing
in the sand. I'm not in an international
airport kicking at an empty box of *Original Russian Vodka*.
Didn't even draw blood from my face with a broken bottle. I do not carry
my brother. Or any other of the dead. I do not carry
myself. The waves bite. There's not even a thimbleful of candor.
Your eye sees me dancing on the edge of imprecations.
The sand is the green kind, sea sand. Three
sleep; four speak to you; two thousand break to pieces. Just one,
between the glass of the tropics and the sperm from Monday, vociferates—
and that one is on vacation, is on vacation.

I'm not me. You aren't you. They're not four or three.
Or two thousand. Or the possible data from the Bishop,
our computer. Also you are looking for enemies,

y hay quien te usurpa el nombre. (Alguien lo cumplirá—
se está cumpliendo, se cumplió.) Realmente no te molesta
la frivolidad metafísica de Scheler, Nadie, ¡Atón! ¡Atón!—
Oh, aquellos tres viejitos del basural cantando, ay,
danza extraña; mira sus marcapasos. Míralos. No al *héros*
Saturday Evening Post. También se gasta mi cigarrillo—
y miente. Al final uno vuelve a cavar otro túnel—uno,
viejo topo corrupto, Franz, al arca, al arca, Franz.

Para Efraín Rodríguez

and there's someone who usurps your name. (Someone will fulfill it—
is fulfilling it, did fulfill it.) Really the metaphysical frivolity
of Scheler, No One, doesn't bother you, Aten! Aten!—
Oh, those three old guys from the dump singing, o,
strange dance; look at their pacemakers. Look at them. Not the A.A. *heroes*
in the *Saturday Evening Post*. My cigarette is burning out too—
and it tells lies. In the end one goes back to dig another tunnel—one,
old corrupt mole, Franz, to the ark, to the ark, Franz.

For Efraín Rodríguez

Notas sobre el texto original

El poemario *Abuso de confianza* se publicó en Santiago de Chile en la editorial Kipus 21 en diciembre de 1992. Posteriormente volvió a publicarse en Cuba, finalmente formando parte de la *Poesía completa* de Escobar (Ediciones UNIÓN, 2006).

Estas ediciones adolecen de numerosas discrepancias. A modo de ejemplo, en el índice mismo los editores adoptan modos distintos en el uso de las mayúsculas. Dentro de los poemas hay discrepancias sueltas en cuanto a palabras, usos de repetición, encabalgamiento, y un elemento gráfico que aparece en la edición chilena (cajas rectangulares vacías que evocan espacio en blanco). Ambas ediciones tienen errores. Generalmente, para esta edición bilingüe, he elegido seguir la edición cubana cuando se producían dichas discrepancias. Una excepción a esta práctica fue el uso de las cursivas en "Mente rota." La edición chilena hace un uso más frecuente de las cursivas, y me incliné por esta opción porque acentúa el conceptualismo teatral de Escobar.

Una contradicción mayor entre las versiones chilena y cubana se produce al final del poema, "Los cuatro cuentos." Una sola letra crea significados completamente opuestos entre las dos ediciones. La versión chilena concluye con la declaración "Ya yo estoy muerto". La cubana dice claramente – y casi como una respuesta – "Ya no estoy muerto". Una vez más he optado por la versión cubana para mantener mayor consistencia con esa edición y también porque prefiero la conclusión más sorprendente en dicho poema.

Kristin Dykstra

Notes on the Original Text

The Spanish-language collection *Abuso de confianza* was published in Santiago, Chile, by Kipus 21 Editora in December 1992. It would be republished in Cuba, where it was eventually incorporated into the Poesía completa, or collection of Escobar's *Complete Poetry*, released by Ediciones UNIÓN in 2006.

Many details in the presentation of the Spanish differ between these editions. In the table of contents alone, for example, the editors adopted different systems of capitalization. Within the poems there are occasional discrepancies in phrasing, uses of repetition, enjambment, and a graphic element that appears in the Chilean edition (empty rectangular boxes that signal white space). Each edition contains some errors. For this bilingual edition I mostly chose to follow the practices of the 2006 Cuban version where the two differ. One exception is in the use of italics in "Mente rota/ Broken mind": italics appear more often in the Chilean edition, and I restored them because they enhance Escobar's theatrical conceptualism.

A major contradiction between the Chilean and Cuban offerings appears at the end of "Los cuatro cuentos." One single letter creates opposite meanings out of the Chilean and Cuban editions of this poem. The Chilean edition concludes with the statement, "Ya yo estoy muerto" (I am already dead). The Cuban edition declares—as if in firm reply—"Ya no estoy muerto" (I'm not dead anymore). Again I follow the Cuban edition, both in order to be more consistent and because I prefer its more surprising conclusion.

Kristin Dykstra

In 1989, Martin Majoor designed a groundbreaking serif typeface, FF Scala, for the Vredenburg Music Center in Utrecht. In 1991, FontFont released the face as FF Scala. It appears in this book, along with its sans serif version for titles.